What People Are Saying About
From Fear to Faith

Scripture tells us "the beginning of wisdom is fear of the LORD." But what kind of fear and how much fear is too much when it comes to our relationship with God and our efforts to live as Catholic Christians? Drawing from his own personal struggles, Gary Zimak combines experience with solid Church teaching and God's word to address these important questions and more in his book. Given the many challenges facing believers today, this book is a must-have for those who are serious about becoming the people the Lord wants them to be.

> **Teresa Tomeo** (teresatomeo.com), motivational speaker, best-selling author, syndicated Catholic talk-show host

Jesus said fear is useless, and what is needed is trust. Yet how do we move from ordinary life in our age of anxiety to that trusting life of faith? Gary Zimak shows the way in steps even I can follow. You'll come to treasure this book, but don't just keep it to yourself. Buy copies for your friends and family members who need it.

> **Mike Aquilina**, EWTN television host and author or editor of more than forty books on Catholic history, doctrine, and devotion

You'll laugh, you'll experience relief, and your faith will become fortified. *From Fear to Faith: A Worrier's Guide to Discovering Peace* is a unique book guaranteed to put you at ease. Through a heartfelt, conversational approach, Gary Zimak underscores the necessity of encountering Jesus to fully experience the joy of the Gospel. Zimak offers solid, no-nonsense proof of why worrying is detrimental to the health of body and soul and provides a doable step-by-step plan to overcome worry and fear. Practical reminders and reflection points complete each chapter. Great for laity, priests, religious, and ministries—highly recommended!

Donna-Marie Cooper O'Boyle (donnacooperoboyle. com), EWTN television host, speaker, and author of *The Miraculous Medal: Stories, Prayers, and Devotions,* and *Catholic Mom's Cafe: 5-Minute Retreats for Every Day of the Year*

Gary Zimak has created a masterpiece. This book is a sincere, energetic, and practical source of encouragement to all of us who have ever struggled with self-doubt or fear. It's an indispensable resource for the journey of our lives. Read it and allow yourself to be transformed. The peace of the Lord awaits!

Kevin Lowry, chief operating officer of Coming Home Network International and author of *Faith at Work: Finding Purpose Beyond the Paycheck*

One of my favorite passages in the New Testament is when Jesus tells his apostles: "In the world you will have trouble, but take courage, I have conquered the world" (John 16:33). There is no doubt, as Jesus affirms, that we live in a troubled world that could give us much to worry about. Yet our faith in the promises of Christ gives us the ability to overcome our fears and anxieties. In *From Fear to Faith*, Gary Zimak gives both practical advice and biblical examples to help us have total confidence and trust in the goodness of our loving God. I highly recommend this book to all!

Donald Calloway, MIC, author of *Marian Gems: Daily Wisdom on Our Lady* and other books

From Fear to Faith is an insightful and challenging look at how fear keeps us "running in place," afraid to take that next step toward greatness. The reader will discover how worry and fear produce lukewarm Catholics, rather than spirit-filled proclaimers of the Gospel. With vivid clarity, honesty and thoughtfulness, Gary Zimak draws from sacred Scripture, practical wisdom, endearing personal stories, and timeless devotions to show how unwavering trust in God's love casts out all fear, heals wounds of sin and division, and opens our hearts to God's will in our lives. This book is a must-read for anyone who is stuck in the abyss of fear and yearns to ascend toward the summit of enduring peace.

Deacon Harold Burke-Sivers, EWTN series host, author, and director of Dynamicdeacon.com

In conversational style, Gary masterfully weaves his personal experience of anxiety and fear with the gifts of the Catholic Church to forge a path to healing. He shows us how to, as he says, "let Jesus do most of the work." Whether you suffer with anxiety or fear, are a health-care provider or a priest or religious seeking resources, this book is for you!

Staci Gulino, MSN, APRN, PMHNP-BC, psychiatric mental health nurse practitioner, host of *Faith & Good Counsel* and *Wake Up Louisiana* on Catholic Community Radio

FROM FEAR TO Faith

A Worrier's Guide to Discovering Peace

FROM FEAR TO *Faith*

A Worrier's Guide to Discovering Peace

Gary Zimak

Liguori
LIGUORI, MISSOURI

Imprimi Potest:
Harry Grile, CSsR, Provincial
Denver Province, The Redemptorists

Published by Liguori Publications
Liguori, Missouri 63057

To order, visit Liguori.org or call 800-325-9521

Library of Congress Cataloging-in-Publication Data

Zimak, Gary.
  From fear to faith : a worrier's guide to discovering peace / Gary E. Zimak.—First Edition.
  pages cm
  1. Fear—Religious aspects—Christianity. 2. Worry—Religious aspects—Christianity.
  3. Peace—Religious aspects—Christianity. 4. Catholic Church—Doctrines. I. Title.
  BV4908.5.Z56 2014
  248.4—dc23

                                    2014018796

p ISBN 978-0-7648-2492-0
e ISBN 978-0-7648-6938-9

Liguori Publications, a nonprofit corporation, is an apostolate of The Redemptorists. To learn more about The Redemptorists, visit Redemptorists.com.

Printed in the United States of America
18 17 16 15 14 / 5 4 3 2 1
First Edition

Dedication

To my wife, Eileen: This book (and all of my work) would not be possible without your constant support. Thank you for your friendship and unconditional love. You are my greatest blessing, and I'm extremely grateful to the Lord for sending you into my life.

I love you, Honey!

Contents

Introduction

"Why are you terrified?
Do you not yet have faith?"

MARK 4:40

Jesus' questions, directed to his disciples in midst of a storm at sea, could easily be directed to each of us whenever we are worried. Considering that it comes from the lips of Christ, these questions could understandably prove frightening or even depressing. In reality, however, it's a good idea to think about these words in a positive way. After all, if our faith is lacking, we should be aware of it so we can take steps to correct the problem.

Like many of you, I am traveling the road that leads from fear to faith. I definitely know what it's like to live in fear, always afraid that something bad is going to happen to me or my loved ones. Conversely, I also know the peace that results from trusting in God's providence. I'd be willing to bet that you have encountered similar experiences. Furthermore, I'll go out on a limb and guess that you'd prefer to walk by faith rather than by fear. What's stopping us then? Even though we don't want to live in fear, many of us are worriers by nature. Speaking from personal experience, this is something that can be overcome with some work on our part and lots of help from the Lord!

As discussed in my first book, *A Worrier's Guide to the Bible: 50 Verses to Ease Anxieties,* I have a tendency to worry. Ever since I was a young child, I've been prone to anxiety. And not just a little anxiety, but *a lot* of anxiety! I'm not sure precisely when this tendency started, but I know that when I was in the first grade I began to worry that my father or mother would die suddenly. Although I had no basis for this fear (my parents were healthy), it was exacerbated when a second-grade classmate's father passed away unexpectedly. While that fear remained with me, another one was added when I was in the fourth grade. While reading a book on the life of President Theodore Roosevelt, I discovered he developed asthma at a young age. Once that seed was planted in my worry-prone mind, I started to experience some breathing difficulties. As I continued to worry about this, the symptoms seemed to increase. As you can probably guess, a subsequent visit to the doctor revealed no underlying illness and, interestingly, the symptoms vanished once I got a clean bill of health. As the years passed, the fear about asthma was replaced by concerns about diabetes, leukemia, and brain tumors. The pattern was similar. I'd worry about my imaginary disease, convince my parents to take me to the doctor, and feel relief once the tests came back negative. Once I graduated from college and happened to feel some fluttering in my chest, I moved on to worrying about having a heart attack. At this point, things started to get really ugly for me.

Over the next several years, I experienced numerous panic attacks. I ended up in the emergency room on multiple occasions, certain that I was having a heart attack. Eventually a battery of tests revealed that I had no underlying heart problems. And my doctor prescribed medication as a temporary solution. Although the prescription helped my panic attacks, it caused other problems. The pills turned me into an apathetic zombie, which made it difficult to function in my job as a computer programmer.

Reluctant to put me on medication on a regular basis, my doctor suggested I pursue some kind of meditation. His suggestion made me uneasy. While my faith wasn't especially strong at the time, I did go to Mass each week, and I remember thinking I should be able to control my anxiety through my relationship with God. Although I didn't pursue this idea (it was a fleeting thought), a seed was planted. It was a seed that would continue to grow for the next several years. In the meantime, I managed to convince myself that I was healthy. When I began to doubt, I remembered the medical tests and was able to relax. After several months, I was able to stop taking medicine, and the panic attacks remained more or less under control for the next several years, but my anxiety never went away. Sadly, I accepted that this was how I was built, and I might as well get used to it.

I eventually got married, had children, and lived a relatively uneventful life. In late 2004, however, I started feeling extremely nauseous and began losing weight. My doctor was concerned and ordered tests. It was discovered I had some enlarged lymph nodes in my abdomen. A subsequent visit to a hematologist led to a possible diagnosis of lymphoma, but it couldn't be confirmed for several months. That's all I needed to hear. Fearing I was dying and would soon be meeting the Lord (once a hypochondriac, always a hypochondriac!), I finally decided to embrace my Catholic faith. Until this time, I was a lukewarm Catholic. I went to Mass on Sunday, but that was it. Now it was time to start getting to know the Lord for real! I was surprised to find that I was able to feel great peace even though I was in the midst of a storm. As I continued to pray and immerse myself in Catholic teaching, the peace increased. Eventually the symptoms disappeared (with no definitive diagnosis), but my life was forever changed. Through my prayers, reading the Bible, and studying the teachings of the Church, I now had a genuine, personal relationship with Jesus Christ, and I never wanted to return to my old, lukewarm way of life. After many years of living in fear, I finally understood that having a deep, personal relationship with Jesus is the ultimate weapon against fear.

As my love for the Lord increased, I founded the apostolate Following the Truth with the purpose of spreading the good news of the Catholic faith. My desire was not only to share facts about what Catholics believe but to help people develop a personal relationship with Christ. I understood that all the facts

in the world don't mean a thing if we don't know Jesus personally. After reaching out in this manner for a few years, I felt the
Holy Spirit prompting me to focus on a group of individuals
who desperately needed to hear this message: my fellow worriers. After the release of *A Worrier's Guide to the Bible,* I began
speaking extensively about the concept of breaking free from
anxiety. These talks continue to this day and have become my
most requested topic. When I speak at parishes and conferences,
I focus on Bible verses that remind us that God doesn't want us
to worry. More importantly, I provide my audience with a simple
plan for leaving anxiety behind and moving from fear to faith.
As I've traveled the country presenting this well-received advice,
a common question has arisen:

"Is this written down anywhere?"

I'm pleased to say that it is now. You're holding it in your hands!
This book will help you leave your fear behind and run into the
open arms of Jesus. It will provide you with a step-by-step plan
for moving from fear to faith. While it's a journey that we'd all
like to make, we're often unsure how to proceed. In the pages
that follow, you'll learn why fear can be dangerous if not handled
correctly, explore some biblical examples of faith in action, and
learn how to make the journey from fear to faith in simple and
achievable steps. At the end of each chapter, I have included three
sections designed to help you:

1. **Remember:** Focus on the message.

2. **Reflect:** Apply it to your life.

3. **Respond:** Offer a prayer in response. Of course, you're always
   free to speak to the Lord in your own words, but these prayers
   may help get you started.

Overcoming anxiety is a big job and requires a great deal of
effort. If you're like me, you've probably tried and failed many
times. If you search the internet, you will find many step-by-step

approaches for eliminating worry from your life. Unfortunately, the majority of them put the entire burden on us. There are a few reasons why this is not a good idea. For one thing, it's not easy for us to just stop worrying, especially if we're anxious by nature. It truly is a big job. More important, these I-can-do-it methods completely remove Christ from the equation. The steps I present in this book do just the opposite. *I recommend we let Jesus do* most *of the work.* Not only is it just about impossible to overcome anxiety without getting to know Jesus personally, but it's also a bad idea. If you have been unable to stop worrying on your own, be thankful.

Some people manage to stop worrying by using one of the aforementioned mind-over-matter approaches, but they do it without the Lord's help. While these people may be able to give up worrying (at least until they're faced with a catastrophe), doing so without growing closer to Jesus does not increase their chances of spending eternity with him. The method I'm presenting here is based on a deep, personal relationship with Christ. Your anxiety will decrease as you grow closer to him. I will devote an entire chapter to this concept, but for now be aware that a meaningful relationship with the Lord cannot flourish without daily prayer. If we expect to grow in faith (and leave our worries behind), we have to speak to the Lord every day.

In his apostolic letter, *Porta Fidei,* Pope Benedict XVI reminds us that the journey of faith will last for the rest of our lives. While this is certainly true, you will begin to see results as soon as you set out on that journey. In his apostolic exhortation, *Evangelii Gaudium,* Pope Francis begins by stating that the "joy of the gospel" fills the hearts of those who encounter Jesus. By following the techniques described in this book, you'll begin to feel more peaceful as your relationship with the Lord grows and you'll trust more deeply in his providence. I also want to point out that, although these steps are simple to understand, they do involve some work. It's not easy for us to trust God with our life, especially when we've become accustomed to being in control. Turning your life (and your worries) over to the Lord can be difficult, but it's something we must do if we want to experience his peace. It's something we can start doing now.

Whether you're tired of living in fear or you simply long for an increased faith, the following chapters will help you grow closer to Christ. Some of you may feel you're not strong enough or lack the discipline necessary to successfully make this journey. Perfect! You and I have a lot in common. In fact, did you know even St. Paul considered himself to be weak? That's right, the man chosen to spread the Good News to the Gentiles not only considered himself to be weak, but he boasted about it (2 Corinthians 11:30). Why? His weakness forced him to rely more on God. This book is designed for those of us who are weak and who have a tendency to worry about almost everything. The beauty of this method is that the Lord will do the heavy lifting. Our job is to do what we can and let him help us. As someone who is living the technique proposed in this book, I can assure you it works. Be prepared to take it one day at a time and be willing to slip up at least once each day. Yes, you read that right. If you're someone who tends to be a worrier, there will still be those times when you fail to trust and begin to worry. No big deal. The closer you get to Jesus, the less frequently these "slip-ups" will occur. More importantly, you'll recognize it when it happens, deal with it, and move on.

Are you ready to get started? Maybe feeling a bit nervous or skeptical? Let's begin by asking the Lord for help. If you're not sure which words to use, I recommend you repeat the words of the father who approached Jesus and asked him to cure his son, who could not speak (Mark 9:14–29). When the Lord said, "Everything is possible to one who has faith," the man's response says it all:

"I do believe, help my unbelief!"

1

What's Wrong With Fear?

What's so bad about being afraid? All people are afraid of something, aren't they? The first thing we should realize is that **there is nothing wrong with fear.** It is an emotion (sometimes referred to as a passion or feeling) and, therefore, morally neutral. As my late mother-in-law used to say, "Feelings are neither right nor wrong."

According to the *Catechism of the Catholic Church (CCC)*:

Feelings or passions are emotions or movements of the sensitive appetite that incline us to act or not to act in regard to something felt or imagined to be good or evil (*CCC* 1763).

In themselves passions are neither good nor evil (*CCC* 1767).

If you've ever been afraid or are experiencing fear now...relax, it's OK. You're in good company! The Bible says Moses, Elijah, David, Mary, Joseph, and Paul were all afraid (Exodus 2:14, 1 Kings 19:3, 1 Chronicles 13:12, Luke 1:30, Matthew 1:20, and Acts 27:24). Look at that list again. If these folks were afraid, you probably feel a little better about yourself, don't you? Remember there's nothing wrong with being afraid for a legitimate reason (more on that in the next chapter). What matters is how we respond to fear.

Responding to Fear

What is fear? Fear occurs when we sense danger or the perceived threat that something bad is about to happen. It can be a useful emotion, especially when it causes us to take action. In fact, fear can be a GOOD thing because it can act as a wake-up call and motivate us to do something. While there is nothing wrong with fear, we can react to it in a harmful way. Let's look at examples to help illustrate negative and positive responses to fear.

Suppose you're walking down a dark, deserted street and you suddenly notice someone following you. You begin to sweat as you realize that you could be attacked. In this instance there is a chance you're overreacting and everything will be fine, but there's also a chance your fears will prove correct. You have two choices. You can choose to continue walking, hope you're overreacting, let your fears run away with you, but essentially do nothing. On the other hand, you can quickly retreat into a busy store, proceed to a crowded intersection, or maybe even cry out for help. By responding to your fear in a proactive way, you spare yourself from potentially becoming a crime statistic. In one case you responded to your fear by doing nothing, letting your fear control you, and in the other case you responded by doing something positive, taking control of a fearful situation.

Next, imagine you're sitting in your living room and are overwhelmed by the smell of smoke. You get up and look in the kitchen to see it is filled with a thick cloud of smoke. How would you respond? Would you sit back down and begin to worry or would you call the fire department and exit the house? It's obvious that one course of action is productive and the other (worrying) is useless.

Looking at fear on a spiritual level, how would you react if you're afraid you won't be able to go to heaven because you have committed several mortal sins? You have two main choices: You can continue worrying and do nothing, or you can go to confession and resolve to lead a holier life. By choosing the productive option (confession and fighting against future temptation), you avail yourself of God's mercy, and eternal happiness in heaven is once again possible for you.

In each of these examples, a positive response to fear produced something good. As a result, we can say that fear can be a good thing. Indeed, it can be a *very* good thing. If you weren't afraid, it's likely that you would have taken no action. Therefore, the emotion of fear can be a great blessing in our lives. When I speak at parishes or conferences, I always remind my audience that it's OK to be afraid. Really...it is! Does that make you feel a little better? It should. Don't be afraid to be afraid. As illustrated in the above examples, fear simply tells us we could be in danger. What matters is what we do with that fear. One response to fear that is always wrong is the act of worrying. Why? Because it doesn't do any good. Need proof? Look at what Jesus said about worrying:

> Therefore I tell you, do not worry about your life, what you will eat [or drink], or about your body, what you will wear. Is not life more than food and the body more than clothing? Look at the birds in the sky; they do not sow or reap, they gather nothing into barns, yet your heavenly Father feeds them. Are not you more important than they? Can any of you by worrying add a single moment to your life-span? Why are you anxious about clothes? Learn from the way the wild flowers grow. They do not work or spin. But I tell you that not even Solomon in all his splendor was clothed like one of them. If God so clothes the grass of the field, which grows today and is thrown into the oven tomorrow, will he not much more provide for you, O you of little faith? So do not worry and say, "What are we to eat?" or "What are we to drink?" or "What are we to wear?" All these things the pagans seek. Your heavenly Father knows that you need them all. But seek first the kingdom (of God)

and his righteousness, and all these things will be given you besides. Do not worry about tomorrow; tomorrow will take care of itself. Sufficient for a day is its own evil (Matthew 6:25–34).

Pretty clear, isn't it? It's difficult to misunderstand Jesus' words. Worrying is useless! Notice that he never denies that we need material (temporal) goods. Instead, he reminds us we shouldn't *worry* about them. That makes all the difference in the world! The Lord is not saying we shouldn't earn a living or prepare for the future. He is saying that we shouldn't sit around and worry about what we will do if this, that, or the other thing happens. Worrying and preparation are different.

Here's another biblical example of an incorrect response to fear. In this case, a young man gets the offer of a lifetime but is too afraid to accept.

Now someone approached him and said, "Teacher, what good must I do to gain eternal life?" he answered him, "Why do you ask me about the good? There is only One who is good. If you wish to enter into life, keep the commandments." He asked him, "Which ones?" And Jesus replied, "You shall not kill; you shall not commit adultery; you shall not steal; you shall not bear false witness; honor your father and your mother"; and "you shall love your neighbor as yourself." The young man said to him, "All of these I have observed. What do I still lack?" Jesus said to him, "If you wish to be perfect, go, sell what you have and give to [the] poor, and you will have treasure in heaven. Then come, follow me." When the young man heard this statement, he went away sad, for he had many possessions (Matthew 19:16–22).

Despite having the desire to follow Jesus and get to heaven, the young man is afraid of the potential consequences. He was not willing to give up his comfortable lifestyle, even if it would lead to eternal life. Shockingly, he walked away from eternal happiness because he was afraid that a deeper relationship with Jesus would not satisfactorily meet all his needs.

Now that we know how NOT to respond to fear, let's look at a biblical example of responding to fear in a positive way:

> He got into a boat and his disciples followed him. Suddenly a violent storm came up on the sea, so that the boat was being swamped by waves; but he was asleep. They came and woke him, saying, "Lord, save us! We are perishing!" He said to them, 'Why are you terrified, O you of little faith?' Then he got up, rebuked the winds and the sea, and there was great calm. The men were amazed and said, "What sort of man is this, whom even the winds and the sea obey?" (Matthew 8:23–27).

We often look at this incident and criticize the disciples for their lack of faith. This is understandable, and Jesus even calls attention to the fact that their faith is weak. However, if we study the details closely, a different picture begins to emerge. There is no doubt that the disciples were overcome with fear, which is understandable due to the violent storm surrounding them. As we have established, fear is a natural reaction to the many "storms" we face in our lives. Instead of simply worrying uselessly, however, the disciples did exactly what they were supposed to do. They went to Jesus for help. In other words, they prayed. And what did Jesus do? He calmed the storm. In addition, he taught them a lesson about the importance of faith. This is a perfect example of how fear can lead us closer to the Lord. When the "storms" in our lives arise (and they will), it's OK to be afraid. What matters most is what we do with that fear. Do we turn to Jesus (as we should) and ask for help or do we worry and ruminate on a multitude of negative outcomes that could potentially occur? One choice will bring us closer to Jesus and allow us to experience his peace. The other option will take us away from him and increase our stress. It's really a no-brainer, isn't it?

The great thing about fear is that it gives us the opportunity to invite Jesus more deeply into our hearts. He longs to be involved in every aspect of our lives, but he will not force himself on us. This Bible verse sums up the situation nicely:

> Behold, I stand at the door and knock. If anyone hears my voice and opens the door, [then] I will enter his house and dine with him, and he with me (Revelation 3:20).

Every time you encounter a problem or experience fear, Jesus is knocking at your door. He wants to come to your assistance and help you. If you are afraid right now, he is at standing at the door of your heart. The choice to answer the door (or not) is up to you. The Lord respects our free will and will allow us to handle our problems alone, if that's what we want. If you're reading this book there is a good chance you're looking for some relief. You've probably realized that your way isn't working and you need some help. Excellent! We'll discuss how you can go about getting that help in future chapters. For now, all you need to do is recognize the great opportunity fear provides. It gives you the chance to "open the door" and TRULY let Christ into your life.

Remember:

1. Fear alerts us that we could be in danger.
2. It's perfectly acceptable to be afraid; fear is just an emotion.
3. Fear can lead us closer to Christ.
4. Worry is an incorrect response to fear. It accomplishes nothing!
5. Fear should not stop us from doing the right thing.

Reflect:

1. How do I typically respond to fear? Do I act or worry?
2. When I'm afraid, do I draw nearer to or turn away from Christ?
3. How has fear helped me?
4. Do I worry excessively about what could happen in my life?
5. Have I ever failed to do something just because of fear, and do I wish I could overcome this limitation?

Respond:

Jesus, help me to trust you with my life. Instead of worrying, grant me the grace to seek your assistance. I know you love me and care about me. Please grant me your peace and allow me to always remain close to you. Amen.

2

Legitimate Fear

In the last chapter, I said it's totally acceptable to be afraid for a legitimate reason. What's up with that? Is there such a thing as illegitimate fear? You better believe there is! Before we begin to look at faith, let's examine the idea of legitimate fear. Why is this necessary? Simple. If we were to look at all of the things we fear, we would realize that most of them pose no real danger and many are completely imaginary. Recognizing this will help us greatly as we make the journey from fear to faith.

In his first inaugural address, President Franklin D. Roosevelt proclaimed the memorable words, "The only thing we have to fear is fear itself." In other words, sometimes our fear can be a bigger danger than the thing we fear. This is especially true when it comes to imaginary problems. We are often afraid when we shouldn't be. The purpose of this chapter is to help us understand that important concept. Let's look at a few examples:

When I speak at parishes, I like to tell my Space Mountain story as an example of what it's like to be afraid. In 1985, before I was married, I visited Walt Disney World with by best friend, Chuck. We planned our vacation a year in advance and had plenty of time to discuss what we would do while we were there.

One day the subject of Space Mountain came up. Space Mountain is an indoor roller coaster at Walt Disney World in Orlando, Florida. For the record, I am afraid of heights and have a weak stomach. As a result, I do not like roller coasters. As the weeks progressed, Space Mountain kept coming up in conversation. Chuck told me it's "a roller coaster in the dark, so it can't be too scary." I started to feel that Chuck was questioning my manhood, so I took the macho approach of pretending that I wanted to ride Space Mountain, too. I also thought that it would be a nice thing to do for my friend. While I was still terrified, I rationalized it might not be too bad if I couldn't see anything. If I was unable to see how high up I was, then I probably wouldn't be afraid. Even though I wasn't fully convinced, I was satisfied that going on the ride wouldn't be too bad and it would allow me to look like a man and help my friend. More importantly, I wouldn't have to worry about it for several more months, so it didn't seem like that big of a deal.

When we arrived at our vacation destination, it was time to face my fear head on. Chuck and I stood in the long line for Space Mountain and my stomach began to feel queasy. As we reached the front of the line, I began to get really annoyed for letting myself get roped into this plan. I said to Chuck, "I hope you're happy that I'm doing this for you!" "For me?" he replied. "I thought I was doing it for you?"

Yes, as it turned out, both of us were scared to death, but neither wanted to admit it! Too late now...it was our turn. Looking back, I was wrong about just how bad an experience it would be. It wasn't bad...it was HORRIBLE! The fact that we were in the dark didn't matter one bit. I knew when we went up, down, sideways, and everything else. I was terrified and convinced my life was coming to an end. And then it was over. When I recall this incident, I realize I learned a valuable lesson. Aside from reminding myself why I don't like roller coasters, I learned something much more important. That lesson? Just because you *feel* you're in extreme danger, you may not be. Although it seemed like my life was going to end on Space Mountain, I was actually safe. If I took the time to think about that fact, I wouldn't have been as frightened. My main mistake was that I reacted to my senses, which told me I was in serious danger. In reality, my senses weren't presenting the true picture.

In the previous chapter, we looked at the biblical account of the storm at sea. The disciples were terrified when the storm began to rock the boat. Were they ever truly in danger? No. Someone (Jesus) was present who could calm the raging sea. The fact that Jesus referred to them as "terrified" indicates they truly believed their lives were in danger, but they were actually safe. Once again, we see a case of how our senses can sometimes fool us into thinking we're in serious danger.

Fear of the Lord

One type of fear that is legitimate and should always be taken seriously is the fear of the Lord. In my book, *Listen to Your Blessed Mother*, I discuss this kind of fear in detail, and it will be helpful to revisit that discussion here. The whole idea of fearing God has become unpopular in the present age, and we've moved toward a kinder, gentler version of the Lord. Unfortunately, that shift in thinking has created many problems in the world and often causes us to believe that sin is no big deal anymore because we're dealing with a "warm and fuzzy" God who really doesn't care if we disobey his commands. While it's true that the Lord will continue to love us no matter how much we sin, there's a little more to it than that.

Here's what the Bible says about fear of the Lord. Throughout Scripture, there are many references to this kind of fear. And rather than it being discouraged, fear of the Lord is always encouraged.

The LORD, your God, shall you fear; him shall you serve, and by his name shall you swear (Deuteronomy 6:13).

But you must fear the LORD and serve him faithfully with all your heart, for you have seen the great things the LORD has done among you (1 Samuel 12:24).

The fear of the LORD is the beginning of wisdom; prudent are all who practice it (Psalm 111:10).

I shall show you whom to fear. Be afraid of the one who after killing has the power to cast into Gehenna; yes, I tell you, be afraid of that one (Luke 12:5).

So what is fear of the Lord and why is it a good thing? Before I delve into that topic, I want to first note that fear of the Lord takes on different shapes. While there are varying degrees of this kind of fear, let's examine the two ends of the spectrum. Although both types of Godly fear are good because they keep us out of trouble, one is definitely more noble than the other. The most basic and primitive form of fear of the Lord is known as servile fear. Basically, this is the fear of getting in trouble. In a worldly sense, this is what stops you from doing 80 MPH in a 35 MPH zone, or what makes you stop browsing the internet when your boss comes over to your desk.

Turning our thoughts to God, at some point in our lives we've all experienced that feeling of "if I commit this sin I'm going to have to answer for it one day." Despite our lack of pure intentions, this kind of fear serves a purpose and occurs often enough to keep us from going to hell. Rather than feeling bad about this less-than-perfect kind of fear, I'm thankful for experiencing it many times in my life. Our fallen human nature often causes us to seek pleasure over doing the right thing. When this happens, a good dose of servile fear (and its reminder of the consequences of sin) can often stop us from committing a serious sin. Again, it may not be perfect, but it sure beats eternal damnation. In addition, this form of fear is often the first step to a greater and more loving relationship with the Lord. For many of us, it was our initial attempt at getting closer to God.

The other, purest form of fear of the Lord is filial fear. This occurs when you love God so much that you fear separation from him through sin. With this type of fear, it's sin and not God that scares you. I can offer a simplified example of this from my childhood. When I got in trouble (and it didn't happen much...really!), my biggest concern was that I would let my parents down. The fact that I would be punished was secondary. I loved my mom and dad, and I always wanted to do the right thing. I didn't want to hurt them by doing something that would make them sad. Having this type of feeling about offending God would be an example of filial fear of the Lord. You may know that fear of the Lord is one of the seven gifts of the Holy Spirit. It is not servile fear but filial fear that is considered to be a gift of the Holy Spirit. Although it may still be in seed form (and remain somewhat undeveloped), those of us who have been baptized and confirmed have some degree of this gift present inside of us. Although St. Thomas Aquinas considered fear of the Lord to be the least of the gifts (wisdom is the highest), he emphasized that all of the Holy Spirit's gifts are necessary for salvation. Therefore, we should be thankful for this gift and continually pray for an increase in it and all of the gifts.

Fear: Real or Imaginary?

My goal in this chapter is to help you understand that sometimes we're afraid when we're actually not in danger. If we can determine when this is the case, we can save ourselves a great deal of stress and aggravation. We still have the rest of this book to discuss techniques for moving from fear to faith, but if we can easily get rid of some unnecessary and illegitimate fear, why not go for it? With that in mind, how can we determine when we're really in danger? It can be a little tricky, but here are two questions we can (and should) ask ourselves when we are afraid.

Is there anything else I can do? If the answer is "no," then it only makes sense that we should let go and turn control over to the Lord. If I'm afraid that I have a serious disease, I can go to the doctor, and I can pray for a favorable outcome. If I'm concerned that my job is in jeopardy, I can update my résumé, begin looking for new employment opportunities, and pray. Once I've prayed and done what I can to minimize the immediate danger, there's a certain freedom that results from knowing I've done my best. Often just realizing this is enough to take away our fear.

Can this affect my salvation? If you have a difficult time with this one, relax. It can take years to sink in. Once we grasp this concept, however, it can bring us great comfort. The reason it's so comforting is that ninety percent of the fear-producing situations in our life will not adversely affect our salvation. If the problem I'm dealing with isn't threatening my salvation, should I really be afraid? After all, we were created to live in heaven for all eternity. This life is only temporary. As we discussed in the previous section, if our salvation is threatened, we should absolutely be concerned. If not, although it's sometimes hard to accept, it shouldn't be as big of a deal. Again, don't feel bad if you have a hard time being unaffected by a cancer diagnosis, job loss, or other frightening issues. This way of thinking doesn't happen overnight. As our relationship with Christ grows and we begin to desire heaven, this mindset begins to develop in us. I'll close this chapter with a powerful Bible verse that asks a very important question:

> The Lord is my light and my salvation; whom should I fear? The Lord is my life's refuge; of whom should I be afraid? (Psalm 27:1).

Remember:

1. Being afraid doesn't always mean we're in danger.
2. Fear of the Lord is a good thing and can help us get to heaven.
3. In its purest sense, fear of the Lord means loving him so much we don't want to hurt him by sinning.
4. We should try to determine whether or not our fears are legitimate.
5. Many of our fears can be eliminated by asking ourselves two questions: Is there anything else I can do? Can this affect my salvation?

Reflect:

1. What are my greatest fears?
2. Am I praying about my fears? Am I doing all I can to minimize them?
3. Am I willing to turn my fears over to the Lord?
4. Can any of my current fears prevent me from getting to heaven?
5. Is my fear of the Lord filial, servile, or a little bit of both?

Respond:

Lord, grant me the grace to recognize when I am afraid for no reason. Help me to trust in your providential care and be willing to turn my problems over to you. Thank you for your willingness to get involved in every aspect of my life. Amen.

3

The Power of Faith

What is faith? Simply, faith is accepting something as fact based on the word of another. If I told you I love coffee and sweets (and I do!), you can choose to believe me or not. Most of you have no way to verify it is a true statement. Although it's a silly example, many of you will have faith in me and choose to believe I'm telling the truth. On the other hand, if I told you I'm the author of *From Fear to Faith: A Worrier's Guide to Discovering Peace*, you don't need to take my word for it. You're holding the book in your hands and can verify it is a true statement. Therefore, no faith is needed.

Although similar in concept, Christian faith has a deeper meaning. According to the *Catechism of the Catholic Church*, faith "involves an assent of the intellect and will to the self-revelation God has made through his deeds and words" (*CCC* 176). When we are baptized, we receive the gift of faith (along with hope and charity), which gives us the capacity to believe that what God has revealed is true. Just as you are free to believe (or not believe) that I like coffee and sweets, you can choose to accept or reject the revelations of the Lord. Because we have free will, we can profess our faith in God or we can choose to reject him. Guess which option is going to bring you more peace?

Before I get specific about moving from fear to faith (and there will be lots of specifics), I thought it would be wise to devote a chapter to our destination—faith. After all, I want to make sure you understand the importance of making this trip. I guarantee that once you see where we're headed, you'll want to get there even more!

Did you ever plan a vacation and spend several months (or even years) dreaming about the destination? This can be especially powerful if you're planning a summer vacation while snow is on the ground! As you view pictures of the beach on the internet, you imagine how great it will feel to be lying on the beach as the warm sun shines on your relaxed body. That mental image helps get you through long days at work and freezing temperatures. Several years ago, my wife and her family planned a Florida vacation. Although everyone in her family wanted to go, they needed to devise a way to save enough money to make it a reality. It was decided that every week, each of her brothers and sisters would put a specified amount of money in a common bank account. Throughout the year, they would hold meetings, report on their financial progress, and look at brochures. This provided the incentive to save the money needed to make the trip. That's what we're doing here. We're going to look at faith and discuss just why it's so important. When you finish reading this chapter, some of you may think, "I wish my faith was stronger," or, "I really want to move from fear to faith." Perfect! That's the point. We'll have plenty of time to discuss how we can get there. For now, let's look at the power of faith and start to desire it in our own lives.

Let's begin by looking at a statement from the *Catechism*. Get ready, because it will blow you away!

> Faith is necessary for salvation. The Lord himself affirms: "He who believes and is baptized will be saved; but he who does not believe will be condemned" (Mark 16:16; *CCC* 183).

Did that get your attention? The Church's position is pretty clear, don't you think? Now, before you begin to panic, think about this. The Church doesn't say a *strong* faith is necessary for us to get to heaven, just that we have faith. As I mentioned, we receive the gift of faith when we are baptized. Weak faith isn't going to disqualify you from being saved and going to heaven. However, we Christians want our faith to be as strong as possible. A strong faith allows Jesus to do amazing things in our lives and bring us great peace. Again, don't worry about how you're going to get there, just focus on how fantastic it will be to have a strong faith.

Here are some biblical examples of what faith can do:

A woman suffering hemorrhages for twelve years came up behind him and touched the tassel on his cloak. She said to herself, "If only I can touch his cloak, I shall be cured." Jesus turned around and saw her, and said, "Courage, daughter! Your faith has saved you." And from that hour the woman was cured (Matthew 9:20–22).

This is an incredible story. Here we have a woman who has been hemorrhaging for twelve years but who believed she would be cured if only she could touch the tassel on the Lord's cloak. How many times do we stop praying when our prayers aren't answered in a month or two? Yet despite twelve years of suffering, this woman believed an encounter with Jesus would be enough to cure her. That's faith! Ultimately, her faith in Christ was what brought about her healing. She believed and, when she had the chance and saw Jesus, she went for it.

Here's another example. One day Jesus and his disciples were leaving Jericho and encountered a blind beggar named Bartimaeus (Mark 10:46–52). He cried out, "Jesus, son of David, have pity on me." When people told Bartimaeus to be quiet, he was unfazed and continued to call out to the Lord. Hearing this, Jesus called the man over and asked:

"What do you want me to do for you?" The blind man replied
to him, "Master, I want to see." Jesus told him, "Go your
way; your faith has saved you." Immediately he received
his sight and followed him on the way (Mark 10:51–52).

Once again, Jesus couldn't be any clearer. Bartimaeus regained
his sight because of his faith. Even the crowd's negativity wasn't
enough to stop him from reaching out to Jesus. I hope that you're
beginning to appreciate just how important faith can be. In order
to drive the point home, let's look at yet another example of what
faith can do:

> At Lystra there was a crippled man, lame from birth, who
> had never walked. He listened to Paul speaking, who looked
> intently at him, saw that he had the faith to be healed, and
> called out in a loud voice, "Stand up straight on your feet."
> He jumped up and began to walk about (Acts 14:8–10).

This passage tells the story of a disabled man who had great
faith. His faith was so strong that St. Paul was able to visibly recognize it. Most of us know people in that category. Their faith is
so strong you can see it just by looking at them. Calling upon the
man's faith, Paul commanded him to stand, and the healing took
place. Why? Once again, it was due to faith. Amazing, isn't it?

I'll bet some of you are getting anxious about increasing your
faith. Am I right? After all, we all need some sort of a physical
or spiritual healing and would like to do what we can to make
it happen. As we look at examples of what faith can do, you may
begin to ask the question, "What can I do to increase my faith?"
It's a common question, one that was posed to Jesus. As was
often the case, he answered in a surprising manner. His answer,
however, is one that should make us feel good even if our faith
isn't what it should be.

And the apostles said to the Lord, "Increase our faith." The Lord replied, "If you have faith the size of a mustard seed, you would say to [this] mulberry tree, 'Be uprooted and planted in the sea,' and it would obey you" (Luke 17:5–6).

While we can take steps to increase our faith (more on that in upcoming chapters), Jesus is reminding us of an easily forgotten fact. Even if our faith is weak (and it may be), it can still accomplish miracles in our lives. Jesus is telling the apostles that even minimal faith can bring about great things. Remember that. This book is about moving from fear to faith, but this piece of information just took a few hundred miles off your journey. You may be much closer than you think. In case you may have missed what Jesus said here, let me repeat it because it's huge. Even if your faith is extremely weak, Jesus can perform big-time miracles in your life, if you give him a chance. Wow!

After you've had a chance to savor that thought for a moment, it's time to come back to earth. As great as faith is, lack of faith or the failure to exercise that faith can get downright ugly. Let's look at some examples that will help us to see what can happen when we don't make use of the gift of faith.

He came to his native place and taught the people in their synagogue. They were astonished and said, "Where did this man get such wisdom and mighty deeds? Is he not the carpenter's son? Is not his mother named Mary and his brothers James, Joseph, Simon, and Judas? Are not his sisters all with us? Where did this man get all this?" And they took offense at him. But Jesus said to them, "A prophet is not without honor except in his native place and in his own house." And he did not work many mighty deeds there because of their lack of faith (Matthew 13:54–58).

If that passage makes you uncomfortable, you're not alone. Remember that the Bible is the inspired word of God, so these are his words to us. The Lord is telling us point-blank that our lack of faith (or the failure to practice that faith) can prevent him from doing mighty deeds in our lives. This includes such things as curing cancer, healing your marriage, bringing you or your loved ones back to the Church, providing you with your dream job, helping you to break free from worry, and more. As I discuss later on, just because we ask God for something doesn't mean we'll necessarily get it, but we could be thwarting the Lord's blessings by failing to believe he can do these works within us.

Here's an example of how a lack of faith can get in the way of a miraculous healing:

> When they came to the crowd a man approached, knelt down before him, and said, "Lord, have pity on my son, for he is a lunatic and suffers severely; often he falls into fire, and often into water. I brought him to your disciples, but they could not cure him." Jesus said in reply, "O faithless and perverse generation, how long will I be with you? How long will I endure you? Bring him here to me." Jesus rebuked him and the demon came out of him, and from that hour the boy was cured. Then the disciples approached Jesus in private and said, "Why could we not drive it out?" he said to them, "Because of your little faith. Amen, I say to you, if you have faith the size of a mustard seed, you will say to this mountain, 'Move from here to there,' and it will move. Nothing will be impossible for you" (Matthew 17: 14–20).

Again, Jesus is clear about what can be accomplished even with a small amount of faith. Look at that last comment. Remember it. Nothing will be impossible for you if you practice your faith. Does that mean the Lord will give you whatever you want, even if it will hurt your chances of getting to heaven? No, but who'd want something that would be harmful to obtaining eternal salvation?

In the next chapter, we'll study the lives of some people who truly put their faith into practice. For now, remember these examples and begin to look forward to how great it will feel once you begin to move away from fear and embrace your faith in Jesus Christ. The mountains will be moving!

Remember:

1. Faith is a gift we receive at baptism.
2. Faith is the ability to believe that what God has revealed is true.
3. We can choose to not respond to the gift of faith.
4. Even the smallest amount of faith is enough to move mountains.
5. Failure to practice our faith can prevent God from doing miracles in our life.

Reflect:

1. Do I believe all things are possible with God?
2. If I believe God can do all things, why do I worry?
3. What would it be like to truly believe my faith could move mountains? How peaceful would I feel?
4. Am I using the faith I have, even if it's weak?
5. What miracles do you need in your life? Do you believe God can perform them?

Respond:

Help me, Jesus, to appreciate the gift of faith. Allow me to see how peaceful I would be if I would put my faith into practice. Grant me the ability to believe that you can do all things and help my confidence in you grow. Amen.

4

Profiles in Faith

In 1955, John F. Kennedy compiled a series of biographies of eight United States patriots that focused on their acts of bravery. The book, *Profiles in Courage,* won a Pulitzer Prize in 1957 and is generally regarded as a classic. In this chapter, let's take a similar approach and look at the faith of several Old Testament personalities. Fortunately, much of the work has already been done for me and is contained in the pages of the Bible. The eleventh chapter of the Letter to the Hebrews is devoted to this very subject and provides some excellent examples of what it means to *live* our faith. While I recommend you spend time reading Hebrews 11 in its entirety, we'll look at some of the highlights. By the time we're finished, I have a feeling you'll have a great appreciation for the power of faith. And, for the record, these individuals are no different than you and me. Every one of us has the capacity to say "yes" and let the Lord work miracles in our lives. These people knew they were weak but trusted God would help them. That's what we're trying to do. Before we look at some Profiles in Faith, let's start by looking at a simple definition of faith:

> Faith is the realization of what is hoped for and evidence of things not seen (Hebrews 11:1).

In short, faith involves believing in something you can't see. Makes sense, doesn't it? If I can see it, no faith is needed.

I touched on the definition of faith in the last chapter, but I'd really like to concentrate on its "invisible" aspect here. A quick story will help illustrate this concept. I live in New Jersey, and every morning after daily Mass I drive my car on a road that runs along the Delaware River. As I look across the water to Pennsylvania, I can see the Philadelphia skyline in the distance. Some mornings, however, are so foggy I can't see anything, including the river. Even though I can't see the city, I know it's there. If I begin to doubt, a quick look at a map will reassure me. In the same way, the Catholic Church teaches me that God exists, even though I can't see him. One thing we need to remember is that sometimes God is going to ask us to "walk by faith, not by sight" (2 Corinthians 5:7). Don't panic; you can do it. We're about to look at some people who truly walked by faith. And, remember, with the Lord's help...so can you!

This biblical narrative begins by looking at Abel and Enoch (Hebrews 11:4–5), both of whom found favor with God because of their faith. In fact, Enoch was such a holy man that he was rewarded with being bodily assumed into heaven (Genesis 5:21–24)! We then hear of Noah, who "warned about what was not yet seen, with reverence built an ark for the salvation of his household" (Hebrews 11:7). While there is no question that each of these men acted on his faith, one of my personal favorites is Abraham. Over and over, Abraham trusted God in ways that never cease to amaze me.

> By faith Abraham obeyed when he was called to go out to a place that he was to receive as an inheritance; he went out, not knowing where he was to go. By faith he sojourned in the promised land as in a foreign country, dwelling in tents with Isaac and Jacob, heirs of the same promise; for he was looking forward to the city with foundations, whose architect and maker is God. By faith he received power to generate, even though he was past the normal age—and

Sarah herself was sterile—for he thought that the one who had made the promise was trustworthy. So it was that there came forth from one man, himself as good as dead, descendants as numerous as the stars in the sky and as countless as the sands on the seashore (Hebrews 11:8–12).

Where do I begin discussing Abraham's story? Throughout his life, when God asked him to do something, he obeyed. Why? Because of his great faith. He trusted that the Lord would provide. He also believed God could do "the impossible." When we read in the above passage that Abraham "went out, not knowing where he was to go," we get insight on how he lived his life. When the Lord called, Abraham listened and obeyed.

The LORD said to Abram: Go forth from your land, your relatives, and from your father's house to a land that I will show you. I will make of you a great nation, and I will bless you; I will make your name great, so that you will be a blessing. I will bless those who bless you and curse those who curse you. All the families of the earth will find blessing in you. Abram went as the LORD directed him, and Lot went with him. Abram was seventy-five years old when he left Haran (Genesis 12:1–4).

Let's examine the passage's details. Abraham (or Abram, as he was known at the time) was seventy-five years old when God asked him to leave Haran (his homeland) and journey to an unknown destination. If we put ourselves in his shoes, how would we have responded to the request? Probably by telling God that we're too old or by asking for further details about the destination, right? It's also possible that we would try to bargain with the Lord and try to get the blessing without having to be inconvenienced and leave our homeland. Abraham didn't ask any questions or hesitate. Instead, he obeyed the Lord's instructions and set out for the Promised Land. If you're familiar with his story, you're aware this won't be the last time Abraham would be asked to trust God:

> Some time afterward, the word of the LORD came to Abram
> in a vision: Do not fear, Abram! I am your shield; I will
> make your reward very great. But Abram said, "Lord GOD,
> what can you give me, if I die childless and have only a
> servant of my household, Eliezer of Damascus?" Abram
> continued, "Look, you have given me no offspring, so a
> servant of my household will be my heir." Then the word
> of the LORD came to him: No, that one will not be your
> heir; your own offspring will be your heir. He took him
> outside and said: Look up at the sky and count the stars,
> if you can. Just so, he added, will your descendants be.
> Abram put his faith in the LORD, who attributed it to him
> as an act of righteousness (Genesis 15:1–6).

Despite the fact that Abraham and Sarah are elderly and
childless, God is now promising they will have many descendants. Pretty hard to believe, isn't it? To us, maybe, but not to
Abraham. Instead of questioning God's plan, Abraham once
again "put his faith in the Lord." Are you starting to get an idea
of just what it means to have faith? Don't you wish you could
have that kind of faith? Hang on, because Abraham's faith is going to look even more impressive. Let's look at one final example
of his amazing faith:

> Some time afterward, God put Abraham to the test and
> said to him: Abraham! "Here I am!" he replied. Then God
> said: Take your son Isaac, your only one, whom you love,
> and go to the land of Moriah. There offer him up as a burnt
> offering on one of the heights that I will point out to you.
> Early the next morning Abraham saddled his donkey, took
> with him two of his servants and his son Isaac, and after
> cutting the wood for the burnt offering, set out for the place
> of which God had told him (Genesis 22:1–3).

After fulfilling his promise and allowing Abraham and Sarah to have a son (Isaac), God asks his faithful servant to do something unimaginable. Abraham is asked to sacrifice the life of his beloved son. You know, the one through whom God promised many descendants. Can you imagine being in Abraham's shoes? At this point, both Abraham and Sarah are about one hundred years old. If God was being truthful about Abraham having numerous descendants, wouldn't it be necessary for Isaac to remain alive? The Letter to the Hebrews explains why Abraham was able to say "yes" to God's request:

> By faith Abraham, when put to the test, offered up Isaac, and he who had received the promises was ready to offer his only son, of whom it was said, "Through Isaac descendants shall bear your name." He reasoned that God was able to raise even from the dead, and he received Isaac back as a symbol (Hebrews 11:17–19).

The final line of that passage tells us all we need to know about Abraham's faith. He trusted God so much that he believed God could raise Isaac from the dead in order to keep his promise. As a result of his faith in the Lord, Abraham was prepared to sacrifice his son's life. While the idea of human sacrifice sounds repulsive and barbaric to us (remember, people thought differently several thousand years ago), we shouldn't let it distract us from the incredible faith necessary to submit to such a plan. The reason Abraham didn't flinch is because he believed God would make good on his promise. That's what happened. Just before Abraham killed Isaac, the angel of the Lord called out to him and stopped him from going through with the act (Genesis 22:11–12). Essentially this was a test, and Abraham passed with flying colors.

While the remainder of Hebrews 11 discusses Moses, Gideon, Barak, Samson, Jephthah, and others, I think you get the point. Faith in God can allow us to do incredible things. But the choice is up to us. We can choose to trust in God's plan for our lives or we can choose to trust we know best and play it safe.

In the next chapter, we'll get personal and look at what it means to have a personal relationship with Jesus Christ. We hear this phrase used frequently and often dismiss it as an empty cliché or something that's just for Protestants. Wrong! In order for us to fully practice our faith and experience the Lord's peace, everyone (including Catholics!) absolutely, positively MUST have a personal relationship with Jesus Christ. Otherwise, it's not going to be possible to take the required steps. How difficult is it to develop a personal relationship with Christ? It's not difficult at all. What does it involve? Read on. We'll discuss it in detail in the next chapter.

Remember:

1. Faith involves believing in things that are unseen.
2. Abraham trusted God would lead him to the Promised Land.
3. By his willingness to offer Isaac as a sacrifice, Abraham expressed his belief that God could raise Isaac from the dead.
4. Things that make sense to God often don't make sense to us.
5. God always keeps his promises.

Reflect:

1. Do I walk by *faith* or do I walk by *sight*?
2. How would I react if the Lord asked me to leave my home and follow him?
3. Am I willing to follow God's will, even if it involves stepping outside my comfort zone?
4. Do I believe God can bring good out of evil (Romans 8:28)?
5. Is there something the Lord is calling me to do? Do I trust he will help me?

Respond:

As I look at the faith of Abraham, Moses, and other biblical figures, Lord, I ask that you help me to imitate their trust in your providence. Grant me the grace to believe in you, even when your plan doesn't appear to make sense. Amen.

5

Getting Personal

Before we move on to a self-assessment (gulp!), I thought it best to devote a chapter to an important question. In order to move from fear to faith, we must ensure we have a good personal relationship with Jesus Christ. But what does it mean to "have a personal relationship with Jesus?" We hear this expression used all the time, but I'd be willing to bet many of you are unsure what it means. While you probably get the general idea, you may have some specific questions, such as:

+ What is a personal relationship?
+ How do I know if I have a personal relationship with Christ?
+ Is it a good relationship?
+ Why does it matter?
+ How can it get better?

These questions are all common, and I'll address each one. Before I begin, I want to assure you of something. The concept of a personal relationship with Jesus is not complicated. In fact, the idea is so simple that we often overlook its importance. Even though the concept is easy to understand, it's what drives (or fails to drive) our spiritual lives. Without a solid personal relationship with Jesus Christ, you will never be able to move from fear to faith. Even though many Catholics aren't comfortable using the "personal relationship" expression, we need to start using it and start living it. If we expect to experience lasting peace in our lives but aren't willing to work at our relationship with the Lord, we're kidding ourselves. Again, the good news is this isn't rocket science. It's extremely understandable and simple to put into practice. I admit, I used the "personal relationship" expression for a long time before I gave serious thought about what it really meant. I knew it was something good, but I never stopped to think about what it entailed. Let's explore the idea and answer some of the more obvious questions that may arise.

What Is a Personal Relationship?

Before focusing on a personal relationship with Christ, let's start by looking at personal relationships in general. What is a personal relationship? Simply put, it's nothing more than interacting with another person. If I speak to you and you speak to me, it can be said we have a personal relationship.

To better illustrate this concept, it may be helpful to examine a relationship that is not personal. I grew up in Philadelphia and was a big baseball fan. My favorite team was the Phillies (big surprise, right?), and I followed them closely, especially during the 1970s. Not only did I know the names and numbers of the players, but I could also tell you the names of their wives and their pets. To this day, I remember that Larry Bowa's wife was named Sheena and their dog was named Mugsy. I knew all *about* Larry Bowa, Steve Carlton, Mike Schmidt, and Greg Luzinski, but I didn't *know* them. In other words, I didn't have a personal relationship with them.

On the other hand, I have a highly personal relationship with my wife, Eileen, and our daughters, Mary and Elizabeth. I interact with them in some way every day. Since I am blessed to work at home and the girls are homeschooled, we see and speak to one another many times throughout the day. Even when I am traveling I am able to speak to them on the phone. We have a personal relationship.

How Do I Know if I Have a Personal Relationship With Christ?

When a friend asked me this question one day, I was surprised and perplexed at the same time. I was speaking to him about the importance of having a personal relationship with Jesus, and he hit me with what initially sounded like a silly question. As I thought about it, however, I realized I didn't have a good answer. I managed to say something like, "Well, you just know." Wow... way to be insightful, Gary (not)!

After realizing I should know the answer to this question, I spent time thinking about it and discussing the matter with others. While the answer is basically what you would expect, it warrants a closer look. You know you have a personal relationship with Jesus if you speak to him as you would to a real person. That's all there is to it. You speak to Jesus, he speaks to you, he loves you, and you love him in return. That's it! I told you it was simple, didn't I?

Now comes the part only you can answer. Do you have conversations with Jesus? Do you pray? Do you ever attempt to hear him speak? Do you receive the sacraments? Do you read the Bible? If you answer "yes" to any of these questions, it's safe to say you have a personal relationship with Jesus. Great, right? Maybe, maybe not! Just because we have a relationship with Jesus doesn't necessarily mean it's a good relationship.

Is It a Good Relationship?

Not all relationships are created equal. Just because I have a relationship with someone doesn't automatically make it a good relationship. For example, if I work so many hours and have so many hobbies that I'm rarely home, it's likely I don't have a good relationship with my wife and children. If I never visit my elderly parents, it's safe to say our relationship is not good.

The same thing applies to our relationship with Jesus. For many years, I was a lukewarm Catholic. Even though I went to Mass every Sunday, I rarely prayed, never read the Bible, and made little effort to communicate with the Lord. My relationship with Jesus was not good, and it was entirely my fault. I was so concerned with seeking pleasure that I wasn't too interested in anything else. Working on my relationship with the Lord involved effort, which didn't appeal to me. If I'm painting an ugly picture of my spiritual life, it's intentional. My relationship with Christ was not pretty.

How about you? Do you have a good relationship with Jesus? While we'll get into the specifics in the next chapter, it would be a good idea to give some thought to the question now. If your relationship with Christ is as bad as mine was, you'll know right away. If it's not bad, we'll look at ways we can make it better. No matter where we stand in our relationship with Jesus, there is always room for improvement.

Why Does It Matter?

Ultimately, this is the question many of you are going to ask. It's blunt, it's a great question, and it's one you have every right to ask. After all, you're reading this book looking for suggestions on moving from fear to faith. Why is it so important that we have a good personal relationship with Jesus? If we don't know Jesus personally, and I mean REALLY know him personally, we won't be able to love him enough to make this journey. As we attempt to move from fear to faith, there will be potholes and roadblocks. We'll be tempted to quit and return to our old way of life because practicing our faith is difficult. I will tell you from personal experience that you will never successfully move from fear to faith unless you know and love Jesus Christ. It is THAT important!

I love my wife and children very much. They mean so much to me I wouldn't hesitate to put my life in danger in order to protect them. I would not even think twice. On the other hand, I *would* think twice before putting my life on the line for a complete stranger or for someone I don't know well. While I may like the cashier at the local supermarket, I won't be as protective of her as I would of Eileen and the girls. Not only is it human nature, but it's also very appropriate. Even though I'm called to love everyone, I should love the members of my immediate family more than strangers or acquaintances. How does this love develop? It happens through a deep and intimate relationship. When I first met my wife, I knew she was beautiful and had a great personality. As we began dating and grew closer, attraction grew into love. As the years passed, our love grew deeper. The same basic principle applies to our relationship with Jesus. The more we get to know him, the more we'll love him. And as our love for Jesus grows, we'll be more willing to listen to him, sacrifice for him, and trust him with our lives.

How Can It Get Better?

First, here's the good news. No matter how bad a personal relationship you have with Jesus, it can be fixed. Even if it's practically nonexistent? Yes, even if it's practically nonexistent. We've got the rest of the book to discuss ways for this relationship to get better, but for now, just know it can improve.

We're now getting ready to spend time determining where we stand. How is my relationship with the Lord? How is my faith? Do I make decisions based on fear or faith? Am I tired of living in fear? Is anxiety ruining my life? Don't worry; it's not as scary as it sounds. For things to improve, we must first be able to recognize a problem exists. How can we correct a problem if we don't know it exists? If you're skeptical about overcoming your fears, don't be. If I can do it, you can. For now, just answer some questions and then we'll begin our journey...the most important one we'll ever make!

Remember:

1. A personal relationship is nothing more than a relationship with another person.
2. Jesus is a person. I can (and should) have a relationship with him.
3. If I interact with Jesus, (through prayer, reading the Bible, receiving the sacraments), then I have a personal relationship with him.
4. In order to move from fear to faith, we must have a close personal relationship with Jesus.
5. Our relationship with Jesus can always improve, but it requires work on our part.

Reflect:

1. How much would I be willing to sacrifice for my loved ones?
2. How much would I be willing to sacrifice for Jesus?
3. Do I speak (and listen) to Jesus every day?
4. Am I willing to work on my relationship with the Lord?
5. Do I speak to Jesus after receiving him in holy Communion? Do I thank him for allowing me to receive him in the most intimate way possible?

Respond:

Dear Jesus, thank you for wanting to be my friend. I'm sorry I may have been ignoring you, but I will try to do better. Please help me to be aware of your presence throughout the day. I look forward to getting to know you better, and I know that—with your help—I will be able to make the journey from fear to faith. Amen.

6

Packing Up

Before leaving on a trip, it's a good idea to think about what you need to bring with you. But how can you be sure you won't forget something really important? One of the best ways is to create a checklist. This method enables you to list everything you need for your trip and ensure it's packed. In theory, it's a foolproof technique. In reality, however, it can be less than perfect.

Here's what happened the first time I used the checklist method of packing. In the early 1980s (while I was working as a computer programmer for the federal government), I was scheduled to go on a business trip to Washington, DC. I was young, fresh out of college, and not used to traveling. Since it's no secret I have a tendency to be anxious, you can probably understand I was a little nervous about making the trip. One of my biggest concerns was I would forget something I really needed. Therefore, I decided I would compile a checklist containing essential items. One by one I checked off various articles of clothing. Shirts...check. Suits... check. Socks...check. As I entered my car to make the three-hour trip from Philadelphia to Washington, I felt confident and remarkably stress-free.

"Good thing I made the checklist," I said to myself as I began to drive through heavy traffic. About an hour into the journey, I started to get a little anxious and decided to run through my list of essential items in my head one more time. Shirts...got 'em. Suits...you bet. Socks...absolutely. Shoes...*shoes?!* Suddenly, I got a sick feeling in my stomach as I now understood one of the major shortcomings of the checklist method of packing. Just because you've checked off all the items on your list doesn't guarantee that your checklist is complete. I had plenty of time to reflect on this as I turned the car around and began heading back through the same traffic I just passed. It was going to be a longer trip than expected, but at least I realized my mistake before it was too late.

Since we are making a journey from fear to faith, it's only logical that we prepare before we leave. Unlike a business trip or vacation, we won't have to worry about packing clothes or supplies. Instead, we'll need to assess where we stand in our relationship with Jesus and try to identify some of our problem areas. Not only will this help us reach our destination faster, but it will increase our desire for getting there. In order to prevent you from using an incomplete checklist (like me), I'm going to provide one for you. Even better, I'm going to ask for assistance from a very special person. Every item on our list will consist of a direct quote from Jesus! In this list, the Lord will be either asking you a direct question or giving you something to consider. How cool is that? Before we start, however, I need to remind you that the purpose of this exercise is to give you an accurate assessment of where you stand with the Lord. There are no wrong answers, and you shouldn't get discouraged at all. My previous statement still applies: Even if you have no relationship with Jesus, there's no need to panic. That will change by the time you're finished reading this book. In fact, it will change by the time you're finished going through the twenty items on the checklist. Are you ready? Let's start!

✎ Listening to God

1. "Everyone who listens to these words of mine and acts on them will be like a wise man who built his house on rock" (Matthew 7:24).

We hear the words of Jesus frequently. In fact, he's speaking to us now in these twenty statements. How do you react when you hear the Lord speak through the Gospels and through the teachings of his Church? Do you act on them or do you ignore them?

✎ Purpose

2. "What are you looking for?" (John 1:38).

Jesus directed this question to two of John the Baptist's disciples, one of whom was Simon Peter's brother, Andrew. It's a question that needs to be answered before beginning your trip. What are you looking for? Greater peace? To be a better person? To get to know Jesus better? To stop worrying? All of the above?

✎ Weaknesses and Sins

3. "Those who are well do not need a physician, but the sick do. I did not come to call the righteous but sinners" (Mark 2:17).

Do you sometimes feel unworthy to grow close to Jesus because you're too much of a sinner? Are you discouraged because of your weak faith? Do you believe it's impossible to have a close personal relationship with him because you're not good enough? If you answered "yes" to any of these questions, Jesus' words should be very comforting to you. He wants to have a personal relationship with the unworthy, the weak, and the sinners (that's all of us!).

✎ Sincerity

4. "Why do you call me, 'Lord, Lord,' but not do what I command?" (Luke 6:46).

When you pray, do you really mean the words you speak? Do you go to Mass each week but not live your faith outside the walls of the church? How do you treat others, especially those you find annoying? Do you sometimes feel like you're just going through the motions as a Catholic?

✎ Burdens

5. "Come to me, all you who labor and are burdened, and I will give you rest" (Matthew 11:28).

If you're reading this book, there's a good chance you are burdened and could use some rest. Unfortunately, sometimes we feel that growing too close to Jesus will increase our burdens. Jesus disagrees! He assures us that a relationship with him will bring us greater peace and help us deal with our daily problems.

✎ Gratefulness

6. "Ten were cleansed, were they not? Where are the other nine? Has none but this foreigner returned to give thanks to God?" (Luke 17:17–18).

Jesus healed ten lepers, but only one thanked him. Do you thank him for answered prayers or do you just move on to your next request? Are you grateful for the blessings in your life? Have you thanked him for dying on the cross to redeem you?

✎ Shame

7. "Everyone who acknowledges me before others I will acknowledge before my heavenly Father. But whoever denies

me before others, I will deny before my heavenly Father"
(Matthew 10:32–33).

Are you sometimes ashamed to admit you're a Catholic? Do
you speak about Jesus to others? Are you afraid to say grace before
meals in a restaurant?

✎ Prayer

8. "And I tell you, ask and you will receive; seek and you
will find; knock and the door will be opened to you"
(Luke 11:9).

How is your prayer life? Do you ever ask for the graces to stop
worrying or to become a better person? When faced with a crisis,
do you pray or do you worry?

✎ Motivation

9. "For where your treasure is, there also will your heart
be" (Matthew 6:21).

What matters most to you? Possessions? Comfort? Success?
What is your greatest motivation? Do you ever spend time thinking about the joy of heaven? How important is your relationship
with Jesus and the members of your family?

✎ Belief

10. "Unless you people see signs and wonders, you will not
believe" (John 4:48).

Do you need to witness miracles in order to believe in God's
providence? Do you trust that he's there even in the darkness?
Do you try to find him in all circumstances, even when you're
suffering?

✎ Worries

11. "Can any of you by worrying add a single moment to your life-span?" (Matthew 6:27).

What are the benefits of worrying? Does it help you solve your problems? Can it make you feel better? Jesus is telling us that worrying is useless and serves no purpose. Do you find yourself worrying even though you realize it accomplishes nothing? Wouldn't prayer be a more productive use of your time?

✎ Vices

12. "Beware that your hearts do not become drowsy from carousing and drunkenness and the anxieties of daily life, and that day catch you by surprise" (Luke 21:34).

Jesus is speaking about the final judgment here, but it also applies to each day of our lives. Have your daily worries caused you to lose sight of Jesus? Do you turn to prayer when anxious or do you seek relief in worldly things, such as drinking, entertainment, or shopping?

✎ Nourishment

13. "I am the bread of life; whoever comes to me will never hunger, and whoever believes in me will never thirst" (John 6:35).

Do you honestly believe that Jesus is the answer to all of your problems and needs? I know he said it, but do you believe it?

✎ Faith

14. "Do you believe that I can do this?" (Matthew 9:28).

Jesus spoke these words to two blind men who were asking for healing. Think of the most serious problem in your life at this moment and picture yourself taking it to the Lord. Are you confident he can help or do you doubt? If he asked you this question, how would you answer?

✎ Sacrifice

15. Then he said to all, "If anyone wishes to come after me, he must deny himself and take up his cross daily and follow me" (Luke 9:23).

What does it take to be a follower of Christ? Jesus spells it out for us with this powerful statement. How willing are you to practice self-denial and take up your cross daily?

✎ Obedience

16. "If you love me, you will keep my commandments" (John 14:15).

It's one thing to say we love Jesus, but it's another thing to prove that love by doing what he commands. Do you keep the Lord's commandments by obeying all teachings of the Catholic Church?

✎ Trust

17. "Amen, I say to you, whoever does not accept the kingdom of God like a child will not enter it" (Mark 10:15).

When you were a small child, did you trust your parents when they asked you to do something? That's the kind of faith we need if we expect to get to heaven. Do you have that kind of trust in God now?

✎ Silence

18. "My sheep hear my voice; I know them, and they follow me" (John 10:27).

In a world full of distractions, are you able to recognize the voice of the Good Shepherd? Do you make an effort to hear his voice? Do you follow his commands?

✎ Reliance

19. "What is impossible for human beings is possible for God" (Luke 18:27).

The world tells us that certain things are impossible, but Jesus reminds us that all things are possible for him. What are the impossible situations in your life? Do you believe the Lord can do anything, including curing cancer or fixing your biggest problems? Have you asked him to help?

✎ Jesus' Invitation

20. "Follow me" (John 21:19).

Jesus is inviting us to follow him. This is how you will be able to move from fear to faith. Are you willing to follow Jesus every day?

So, how did you do? If you're like me, you now realize just how much you need to make this journey. That's a good thing. Do you know what else is good? You just had a personal encounter with Jesus. You now know what it feels like to be one of those people whose story is documented in the pages of the Bible. So many times we wish we could have lived 2,000 years ago so we could have met and been healed by Jesus. Although it may not feel like it initially, that meeting just took place. You just encountered him through the words of sacred Scripture. The next step is up to you. We are ready to begin our journey from fear to faith. You've heard Jesus invite you to follow him. Are you ready? In the next chapter, we'll pack our bags and be on our way!

Remember:

1. Jesus wants to have a personal relationship with us.
2. We can experience peace even in the midst of our problems.
3. Nothing is impossible with God.
4. Childlike faith implies trusting in God to take care of our needs.
5. Worrying is totally useless.

Reflect:

1. What would my life be like if I didn't worry?
2. Am I afraid to grow too close to Jesus because it might involve additional suffering?
3. Have I asked the Lord to help me with my daily struggles?
4. Do I believe Jesus can fix even my biggest problems?
5. Am I willing to hear and listen to the words of Christ?

Respond:

Thank you for speaking to me, Lord. As usual, your words were eye-opening and challenging. I am tired of living in fear, and I want to grow closer to you. Please grant me the strength to trust you more. Amen.

7

Let's Go!

Well, the day has finally arrived. We're getting ready to "pack our bags" and officially begin the journey from fear to faith. If you're feeling nervous or skeptical, that's perfectly normal. If you're feeling excited, that's normal, too. In fact, I'd be willing to bet that you're feeling a little bit nervous and excited at the same time. The reason for this is because while we're all anxious to move away from our fears and to experience peace, the world constantly reminds us that it isn't possible. The world is wrong! Not only is it possible, but anyone (including you) can achieve that peace. Best of all, that peace can arrive in a hurry...like TODAY! If this sounds too good to be true, it isn't. The key (and I'll continue to mention this because it's critical) to experiencing a deep peace in your daily life is a strong personal relationship with Jesus Christ. That relationship will not only lead you from fear to faith, but it will lead you to eternal life in heaven. I can't emphasize this enough. Do you remember the old bumper sticker: *"No Jesus, No Peace. Know Jesus, Know Peace"*? That statement is absolutely true. Knowing Jesus and having faith in him will bring you peace. How can I be sure? Here's a story.

My battle with anxiety is well-documented. I have written about it in books and mention it frequently in my talks and radio appearances. If people are familiar with my work, they know I am someone who has a tendency to worry...a lot! If I let myself, I have the ability to dream up some wild and far-fetched scenarios that may occur in my life. My mind can conjure up an endless supply of negative outcomes that could easily allow me to worry constantly. I am someone who lived in fear for most of my life. Starting when I was a young child, I have wasted thousands of hours worrying about various real and imaginary problems. I have literally worried myself sick on many occasions. I know what it's like to be a worrier and to live in a constant state of fear. The great news is I also know it is possible to successfully move from fear to faith. I would like to say that I have done it, but that wouldn't be entirely accurate. A more appropriate expression would be to say that I do it every day. We'll get into the specifics in a later chapter, but understand this journey is one you'll probably be making every day of your life. It's generally not going to be a one-time trip. Don't panic! Even if you make the trip every day (or several times each day), it will eventually become easier and take less and less time to complete.

Getting back to my story, as an adult one of my biggest fears has been losing my job. What would happen if I was suddenly laid off? How quickly would I be able to find a new job? How would I support my family if I was unemployed? Would we lose our home? Could I deal with the stress? I was fortunate in that, for the first thirty years of my working career, I never had to deal with unemployment. I had a steady income and, while we weren't wealthy, my family and I never experienced any serious financial problems.

On January 6, 2012, one of my greatest fears was realized as I was laid off from my job. At that time, my wife and I decided I should take a chance and follow what I felt was the Lord's plan for me—full-time work as a Catholic lay evangelist. Although I felt this calling for a few years before the layoff, I didn't know how I could possibly support my family by working full time for the Lord.

This idea becomes even crazier when paired with a decision we made a few months earlier. After much prayer, my wife and I decided we would homeschool our twin daughters, Mary and Elizabeth. As a result, Eileen was not able to work, and I had to be the sole breadwinner for the family. While this was always the case for us (Eileen stopped working when the girls were born), it wasn't that big of a deal when I was making a six-figure annual salary. Now that I wasn't receiving any guaranteed pay, we were dealing with a radically different situation. It's hardly a secret that full-time ministry isn't one of your more lucrative professions, and I wondered if my nerves would be able to survive the uncertainty of working as a full-time Catholic lay evangelist. I have learned that the answer to this question is "yes," and I can honestly say I have never been more peaceful in my life.

After many years of worrying about what might go wrong, I am finally learning to trust in God's providence—and it feels great! Why am I including my story in this chapter? Because I want you to know that if I can successfully make the journey from fear to faith, so can you. Furthermore, once you make the journey, you'll never want to return to your old way of life.

With that in mind, we need to discuss a few things. In order for the techniques described in this book to be successful, a commitment is needed. You have to make a firm decision that you want to move from fear to faith. At this point, there is no need to concern yourself with *how* you're going to do it but rather that you *want* to do it. We'll get to the "hows" in future chapters.

If you get a little nervous when you hear the word "commitment," relax. All you need to do is let Jesus help you move from fear to faith. That's not so bad, is it? It's not up to you to make this trip a success; it's ultimately up to Jesus. He's going to do the hard work. Your job is to simply do what you can and trust him to do the rest. As I mentioned in the introduction, don't be surprised if you slip up and begin to worry. It could easily happen one or more times each day. What's important is that you get back on your feet and try again. Feeling a little better? Great.

I think this would be good time to formalize our commitment. Please read over the following pledge and add your signature and the date. Since it's not lengthy, an even better method would be to write it out on a piece of paper first. Why? You're far more likely to live out your pledge if you formalize it in some way. Now that you're starting to feel a little nervous again, it would probably be a good time for me to assure you I'm not going to ask you to sign your life away. Unfortunately, I can't say that because I'm going to ask you to do just that! By signing the following, you pledge to try (remember, you're not promising you'll never fail) to turn control of your life over to the Lord. In return, he will grant you his peace. More important, living your life in this manner and truly following him will result in eternal happiness with him in heaven. If ever there was a win-win proposition, this is it!

The Worrier Warrior Pledge: From Fear to Faith

Dear Jesus,

On this day, I hereby pledge to try my best to trust you with my life. I am tired of living in fear and desire to have greater faith in you. Please help me to live one day at a time and to turn to you when I am afraid. Whenever I begin to worry, I will try my best to turn to you instead. Even though you have told me that worry is useless and that prayer is always effective, I am weak and often forget your words. If I fail to live out my promise and begin to live in fear, I won't give up. Instead, I will turn to you, ask for the grace to succeed, and try again. Together, I know we can do this, and I look forward to moving from fear to faith.

_____

(Signature)   (Date)

A card like the one on page 72 was inserted in this book. A printable version can be found at:
liguori.org/from-fear-to-faith.html.

Congratulations! You have just taken the first step on the journey from fear to faith. You may want to carry this signed pledge with you and look at it several times during the day, especially when you're tempted to begin worrying. Also, remember you didn't promise you would be successful but rather that you would try. Keeping that in mind will take away much of the pressure. In the chapters to come, we'll discuss simple techniques to keep you on the right path and continue moving forward. For now, however, enjoy the fact you just took an important step on the road to greater peace. Many people never take this step and live their entire lives in fear, not realizing the Lord doesn't want us to be anxious (Matthew 14:27). You are on your way. Get ready to experience the peace that comes from a deep personal relationship with Jesus Christ!

Remember, every day you will be tempted to give up and return to your old way of life. There will be days when you don't feel like praying and occasions when it seems easier to worry than to pray. You will encounter people who try to drag you down, either intentionally or unintentionally. Don't be surprised if Satan himself tempts you with the idea that lasting peace is not possible. Expect these attacks, but don't fall for them. You can experience peace in this life, but you have to keep your eye on Jesus. In the following passage, the Lord is reminding us that once we commit to following him (which will lead to peace), there should be no turning back. As you read his words, try your best to put them into practice. The reward will definitely be worth it.

As they were proceeding on their journey someone said to him, "I will follow you wherever you go." Jesus answered him, "Foxes have dens and birds of the sky have nests, but the Son of Man has nowhere to rest his head." And to another he said, "Follow me." But he replied, "[Lord,] let me go first and bury my father." But he answered him, "Let the dead bury their dead. But you, go and proclaim the kingdom of God." And another said, "I will follow you, Lord, but first let me say farewell to my family at home." [To him] Jesus said, "No one who sets a hand to the plow and looks to what was left behind is fit for the kingdom of God" (Luke 9:57–62).

Before we discuss ways to keep you headed in the right direction, I have a big surprise for you. When we go on a trip, we can sometimes get lonely. This is especially true if we are traveling by ourselves. In order to prevent that from happening, we're going to pick up a special friend who will be making the trip with us. Best of all, not only will this person keep us company, but this individual has a great deal of experience with walking by faith and not by sight. Curious about who it might be? You'll find out in the next chapter!

Remember:

1. It's possible to experience the Lord's peace in our lives today, if we try.
2. Jesus knows we're weak. He only expects us to try to trust him with our lives.
3. If we fail and begin to worry, it's not the end of the world. We should just try again.
4. Our chances to successfully journey from fear to faith increase if we make a formal commitment.
5. Once we decide to follow Jesus and trust him with our lives, we should not look back.

Reflect:

1. How do I feel now that I've made a commitment to trust Jesus with my life?
2. Am I prepared to deal with the feelings of doubt I will encounter? How will I react when I slip up and begin to worry again?
3. Do I truly believe I can experience peace in my life? If not, have I asked Jesus to help me believe?
4. Have I thought about the great things the Lord can do in my life if my trust in him increases?
5. What do I have to lose by turning my life (and my problems) over to Jesus?

Respond:

I am committed to making the trip from fear to faith, Lord. Please help me. Even though I am weak, I know all things are possible with your help. Thank you for reaching out to me and wanting to be involved in my life. I love you! Amen.

8

Picking Up a Special Friend

Well, here we are. Our journey from fear to faith has officially begun. How do you feel so far? While you may not feel any major changes yet, you should take comfort in the fact that you just took a big step toward achieving peace in your life. I can say with total confidence that this journey will bear fruit in your life, but you may have to give it a little time before you feel any big changes. While you'll see some results right away, your peace will grow gradually as your relationship with Jesus improves. As we discussed earlier, the journey from fear to faith is all about growing closer to Christ, and peace will be one of the most tangible fruits of that relationship.

Let's get back to the trip. In the last chapter, I told you that you won't be making this journey alone. That's comforting, isn't it? After all, it's always more fun to travel with someone else. What's even better is when you're traveling with someone who knows the route well. Not only will that person be able to keep you company, but he or she will be able to keep you headed in the right direction. As you can probably guess, it's easy to lose our way on the journey from fear to faith. Life has a way of distracting us and causing us to question if we're on the right road. If we're not careful, we may even be tempted to turn around and head back to our original destination. That's where our companion will help us greatly. So, where do we go to pick up our co-pilot? We're headed back in time, 2,000 years ago, to a hill named Calvary.

In the final chapter of *A Worrier's Guide to The Bible,* I reveal the "Secret Weapon" in the battle against anxiety. This "weapon" can better be described as a gift, one that was given to each of us by Jesus as he was dying on the cross. While we are free to reject his gift, those of us on the journey from fear to faith should not do so. Curious? Here's the deal. Jesus' gift to us is not a thing but a person. This person will be our companion on the journey from fear to faith.

> Standing by the cross of Jesus were his mother and his mother's sister, Mary the wife of Clopas, and Mary of Magdala. When Jesus saw his mother and the disciple whom he loved, he said to his mother, "Woman, behold, your son." Then he said to the disciple, "Behold, your mother." And from that hour the disciple took her into his home (John 19:25–27).

By now, I'm sure you've figured out that Mary, the Mother of Jesus, will be our companion on the journey from fear to faith. While he was suffering in great agony on the cross, Jesus struggled to speak these often-repeated and familiar words. Unfortunately, many people don't realize that not only was the Lord presenting the Apostle John (referred to only as "the disciple") with the gift of a spiritual mother, but he was presenting each of us with the same precious gift. The above passage tells us that John "took her into his home." In other words, he accepted Jesus' gift on that day. How about you? Have you accepted Christ's gift of Mary as your spiritual mother? If not, there's no time like the present! While there are formal ways to do this, such as Total Consecration to Jesus Through Mary [1] (which I highly recommend), enrollment in the brown scapular (again, highly recommended), and investiture

---

[1] For more information, visit: **myconsecration.org**

with the Miraculous Medal (you guessed it, highly recommended as well), you can accept Mary as your spiritual mother in a less formal way. It could be as simple as saying, "Mary, I accept you as my spiritual mother." After this declaration is made, speak with her and get used to praying at least one Hail Mary every day. Since Mary is a real person, we can (and should) have a personal relationship with her.

Why is it so important for us to have a personal relationship with Mary and to accept her as our spiritual mother? The main reason is because she will bring us closer to Jesus and will help us stay on the right track. If you would like to find out more about Mary, specifically her recorded words and appearances in Scripture, I recommend you read my book, *Listen to Your Blessed Mother*. For the time being, however, let's take a brief look at Mary's life and how she can bring us closer to her Son.

The greatest and most reliable source of information about the Blessed Mother's life comes from the Bible. Even though her recorded biblical appearances are few, we can learn a great deal from them. In all of Mary's recorded appearances (with one understandable exception), she always appears with Jesus. The only exception occurs after our Lord ascends into heaven and Mary is praying with the apostles (Acts 1:14). It really is remarkable that, while Jesus was on earth, every time Mary is mentioned in the Bible she is with Jesus. She was with him when he performed his first miracle (John 2:1–12) and also when he took his last breath (John 19:25). The Catholic Church has always maintained that this is not accidental. Saint Louis de Montfort, one of the foremost proponents of Marian devotion, stated numerous times in his writings that those who grow close to Mary will grow close to Jesus. Why? Because where we find Mary, we find Jesus. That's the message that emanates from the Bible and one that we should remember. Let's look at examples of why Mary will make an excellent traveling companion on the journey from fear to faith.

Our first look at Mary in Scripture is when the angel Gabriel appears and informs her she has been chosen to become the mother of the Messiah. She responds, "Behold, I am the hand-maid of the Lord. May it be done to me according to your word" (Luke 1:38). Then Jesus is conceived in her womb and God's promise of a Savior is fulfilled. According to the *Catechism of the Catholic Church:*

> At the announcement that she would give birth to "the Son of the Most High" without knowing man, by the power of the Holy Spirit, Mary responded with the obedience of faith, certain that "with God nothing will be impossible": "Behold, I am the handmaid of the Lord; let it be [done] to me according to your word." Thus, giving her consent to God's word, Mary becomes the mother of Jesus. Espousing the divine will for salvation wholeheartedly, without a single sin to restrain her, she gave herself entirely to the person and to the work of her Son; she did so in order to serve the mystery of redemption with him and dependent on him, by God's grace (*CCC* 494).

Mary responds to an "impossible" request (a virginal motherhood) with a clear "yes." She knows nothing is impossible for God. How many of you feel you'll never be able to stop worrying and learn to trust God? Wouldn't it be great to hang out with someone who knows that it really is possible? Wouldn't it be nice to travel the road of life with someone who can help you live out God's will and ultimately help you get to heaven? Our Blessed Mother is that person.

Mary knows what it's like to walk in darkness and understands the importance of walking by faith and not by sight. When informed she would conceive a child by the power of the Holy Spirit, Mary believes. This is confirmed by her relative Elizabeth, who proclaims, "Blessed are you who believed that what was spoken to you by the Lord would be fulfilled" (Luke 1:45). Since roughly ninety-five percent of our anxiety is caused by the fear of the unknown, can you see the advantage of having the Blessed Mother beside you for the journey from fear to faith? As someone who has "been there, done that," she will be an excellent advisor if any doubt begins to enter our mind.

Our Lady also notices things we might miss. In the wedding at Cana (John 2:1–12), do you recall who first notices that the wine has run out? Surprisingly, it isn't the bride and groom, the head waiter, or even Jesus. It's Mary! Why? Because Mary is a mother, and that's what mothers do. They watch out for their children. As our spiritual mother, Mary is always looking for potential potholes in the road leading from fear to faith (the same road that leads us to Jesus and to heaven). As you navigate the twists and turns in that road—and there are many—you may hear her call out, "Turn here!" More likely, you'll feel your imaginary car start to move in an unlikely direction. It will appear someone has taken control of the steering wheel for you. Guess who that might be?

Need another example from the Bible? In the incident referred to as the Finding in the Temple, Mary and Joseph somehow manage to leave Jesus behind as they return from a visit to Jerusalem (Luke 2:41–52). He remains lost for three days, before the couple returns to Jerusalem to look for him. Finding him in the Temple, Mary exclaims, "Son, why have you done this to us? Your father and I have been looking for you with great anxiety" (Luke 2:48). Did you catch the subtle indication of just how seriously they were searching for him? They were looking "with great anxiety." They weren't just sitting around worrying and hoping Jesus would return home. They were actively doing something to find him and it paid off! Despite the fact that Mary is along for the ride, there will be times when we get out of the car and head down a deserted path. Instead of remaining close to Jesus and following his will, we can proceed in the wrong direction. This can happen in any number of ways. Our problems may become overwhelming, causing us to worry or even to become hopeless. We may even seek comfort in sinful activities, turning our back on the Lord. No matter how hard we try to stay on the road, sometimes we're going to get lost. Instead of feeling defeated, however, we should take comfort that Mary is with us. She knows how to find Jesus, even when we don't. Having her with us will greatly reduce the severity of the wrong turns, and when we realize how far from Jesus we have gotten, Mary will help us to search for him "with great anxiety."

My advice to you now is to sit back, relax, and enjoy the journey from fear to faith. In the next chapter, I'll present an overview of the steps we'll need to complete the journey. The good news is that these steps are not difficult. In fact, you've already completed the most difficult part of the trip. The hardest part of the process is making the decision to embark on the journey. Congratulations! You're already on the road, and you have an extremely capable traveling companion. Oh, by the way, I have another big (and pleasant) surprise for you. I'll reveal the details in the next chapter.

Remember:

1. The journey from fear to faith is all about growing closer to Christ.
2. Mary, our spiritual mother, will accompany us on the journey.
3. Where you find Mary, you will also find Jesus.
4. When we make a "wrong turn" and head away from Jesus, Mary will help us to quickly turn around and head in the right direction.
5. The most difficult part of the journey from fear to faith is deciding to start!

Reflect:

1. How well do I know the Blessed Mother? Do I speak to her daily?
2. Have I accepted Mary as my spiritual mother?
3. Can my relationship with Jesus improve? Do I feel bad about my sins, knowing that they hurt him?
4. Am I willing to let Mary make me into a better person? Will I listen to her advice?
5. How do I react when my conscience tells me I'm heading in the wrong direction? Do I deny it or do I attempt to turn around? Am I more willing to listen now, realizing this might be Mary's way of helping me stay on the right path?

Respond:

Dear Blessed Mother Mary, thank you for your willingness to be my spiritual mother. Please stay with me on the journey from fear to faith. When I am tempted to make a wrong turn, I ask you to take the wheel and get me back on the road. Please take me by the hand and allow me to grow closer to Jesus each day. Amen.

9

On the Road!

"Are we there yet?"

Anyone who has taken a trip with young children is familiar with this question. And although those of us who are parents can find it a bit annoying, it's actually a reasonable question. When we set out on a trip with our kids, we generally have an idea of how much time it will take to arrive at our destination. On the other hand, young children often have no idea of how long the ride will last. Since the Lord calls us to be childlike in our faith (as discussed in chapter 6), and most of us are traveling to this destination for the first time, it's totally appropriate that we would ask this question. In this chapter, I'll attempt to answer the question, and I'll give you an overview of the stops we'll make along the way. In case you're wondering, each stop is designed to improve the odds of reaching your destination (greater faith in Jesus) and getting you there as quickly as possible.

OK, where are we and how long will this trip take? Well, I have good news and bad news. I'm going to assume you want the bad news first. Here it is. I can't say for sure how long the journey from fear to faith will take. It will be different for every person. As far as bad news goes, that's really not so bad, right? Before I reveal the good news, let me assure you that it's good news. Even though I can't tell you with certainty just how long your personal journey from fear to faith will take, the good news is that you're much closer than you think! While I'm sure you would agree this is good news, you're probably wondering why you still feel so anxious. Don't worry. Even though you might not feel as peaceful as you'd like, you're really not that far from your destination.

In order to better understand the distance of the journey, we need to restate our goal. This book provides directions for making the journey from fear to faith. It is a guide to moving away from anxiety and moving toward greater faith in Jesus. As I've stated several times previously, our anxiety level will move inversely proportional to our relationship with Jesus. Whoa, what's with the jargon, Gary? Sorry, I couldn't resist the chance to use a fancy term. This simply means that the closer we get to Jesus, the less we will worry. If you're looking for one takeaway from this book, let that be it. Jesus is the answer to all your problems. As you grow closer to him, your peace will improve dramatically.

While our immediate goal is to stop worrying and feel peaceful, our ultimate goal is to grow closer to Christ, have greater faith in him, and live with him forever in heaven. Now, getting back to the good news, let's examine a few facts that back up my statement that you're closer than you realize. In chapter 3, I discussed what happened when the apostles asked Jesus to increase their faith. His response is one that should give us great hope: "If you have faith the size of a mustard seed, you would say to [this] mulberry tree, 'Be uprooted and planted in the sea,' and it would obey you" (Luke 17:6).

Before we start asking for more faith, are we using the little faith we already possess? It's great to ask the Lord to increase our faith, but what difference will it make if we're never going to use it? Jesus is reminding the apostles that, even with faith as small as a mustard seed, they will be able to do great things. I stated this earlier, but it bears repeating now that we're on the journey. This makes the journey from fear to faith a lot shorter. If you have any kind of faith at all (and, if you were baptized, you have received the gift of faith), you can start using it today and great things can happen! We'll discuss how in the following chapters. For now, take comfort in the fact that great changes can take place in your life soon. While those changes will certainly involve a greater feeling of peace, you may be surprised to see some of the other miracles the Lord has in store for you!

Another fact that can shave some time off your trip is the fact that the Blessed Mother is riding with you. In the last chapter, we noted that Jesus is always found with Mary. Since you've asked Mary to accompany you, guess what that means? You guessed it. Jesus is really close to you as well. And since this journey from fear to faith is all about getting closer to Jesus, you're already "in the ballpark." While that is a comforting thought, it shouldn't cause us to stop trying to grow closer to the Lord. We should work on our relationship with Jesus every day and continually try to love him more. Even though I've been living with my wife for nearly twenty years, our relationship is deeper now than it was when we got married. Being close in proximity, however, doesn't automatically mean we are close personally. But if the proximity isn't there, it would be difficult for our relationship to grow. Therefore, the fact that we live together and speak with one another daily helps us grow closer. Your relationship with the Lord can grow in the same way.

Remember the big surprise I noted in the last chapter? Look in the rear-view mirror of your imaginary car and see if you notice anything. Are you surprised to see the Blessed Mother is now riding in the back seat of your car? Does that make you nervous? Just a short while ago, she was your co-pilot and sitting beside you. What gives? Don't worry, you can relax. Picture Mary putting her hand gently on your shoulder (don't take your eyes of the road) and asking you to turn your head briefly to your right (you might want to pull over first!). Now do you understand why our Lady has moved to the back seat? Remember when I told you that wherever Mary is, Jesus is very close by? I'll bet you didn't realize just how close he is. You guessed it. Jesus is now sitting in the front seat with you. As you continue your journey from fear to faith, both Jesus and Mary will be along for the ride. Your job is to let them help you keep the car on the road.

Don't feel bad if your head is spinning; I have dropped some bombshells on you in this chapter. The good news is that you are much closer to your destination than you realized and you have everyone in the car you need. All that stands between anxiety and peace is you! Your actions can and will make the difference. We've already established that you have the desire to change (remember the pledge in chapter 7?) Second, Jesus is with you and is waiting for you to grow closer to him on a personal level. Third, Mary is also with you and wants to get to know you better. She also wants to help the relationship between Jesus and you grow deeper. You even have the faith (even if it's weak) that will allow you to start trusting more. What's missing? All that's missing is some behavior modification on your part. Sounds psychological, doesn't it? In reality it's a simple concept. In order to complete the journey, you just have to change some of the negative habits that are dragging you down. Don't worry, we'll go through these changes in detail, and they aren't difficult. In fact, you'll be surprised when you see just how simple they are.

I've come up with five steps that will enable you to complete the journey from fear to faith. That's all there is to it! Unfortunately, even though these steps are easy to understand and not all that complicated, they are sometimes difficult to put into practice. The good news is you'll be getting plenty of help from your traveling companions. I'll devote a chapter to each of these steps, but let's take a quick look at them here. In order to make these steps easier to remember, I've given them a name: **the Five P's of Peace.** When put into practice, the Five P's will truly bring you PEACE! Here are the steps, along with a brief description of each:

1. **Prepare:** Do what you can to solve your problems.

2. **Present:** Focus on the present; don't worry about the future.

3. **Pray:** Speak to the Lord each day.

4. **Participate:** Take advantage of the Church's gifts, including the Bible, the sacraments, and Eucharistic Adoration.

5. **Prize:** Keep your eye on the prize...focus on heaven!

Although I've been referring to the process of moving from fear to faith as a "journey," it could also be called a "battle." While it sounds a little ominous (although it really isn't), using this term implies we need to exert some effort...and we do! With these five steps and the help of our traveling companions (Jesus and Mary), anyone can win this battle. Yes, even those who are weak. As I mentioned earlier, I also am a weak person, and there is no way I could break free from anxiety on my own. I need LOTS of help and simple, easy-to-follow steps. That's what this approach provides. Whenever I begin to feel I'm too weak to overcome my anxiety, I turn to the words of someone else who thought he was weak. If you feel the same way about yourself, I recommend you keep this Bible passage in mind:

> Therefore, that I might not become too elated, a thorn in the flesh was given to me, an angel of Satan, to beat me, to keep me from being too elated. Three times I begged the Lord about this, that it might leave me, but he said to me, "My grace is sufficient for you, for power is made perfect in weakness." I will rather boast most gladly of my weaknesses, in order that the power of Christ may dwell with me. Therefore, I am content with weaknesses,

insults, hardships, persecutions, and constraints, for the sake of Christ; for when I am weak, then I am strong (2 Corinthians 12:7–10).

Saint Paul concluded that it's OK to have weaknesses. Everyone is weak in some way. The beautiful thing about letting the Lord help us overcome anxiety is that he does most of the work. While we are still expected to do what we can, Jesus will take our efforts and multiply them greatly. The problem with many secular "overcoming anxiety" methods is that they don't include God in the mix. If I'm someone who lives in fear and worries about everything, there's a good chance I'm not strong enough to follow the steps needed to break free from anxiety. That's why we need the help of Jesus and the Blessed Mother. Hang in there and be confident that you will successfully arrive at your destination. With the Lord's help (and some easy-to-follow steps), you will be able to move from fear to faith. If you need some additional encouragement, recall the words the angel Gabriel spoke to Mary:

"...Nothing will be impossible for God" (Luke 1:37).

Remember:

1. Not only does Mary accompany us on the journey from fear to faith, but so does Jesus.
2. Even the smallest amount of faith is enough to see miracles in your life...if you use it.
3. Breaking free from worry can accurately be called a "battle," but it is a winnable battle.
4. You do not have to be strong to overcome anxiety; God's grace will allow you to succeed.
5. If followed, **the 5 P's (Prepare, Present, Pray, Participate, Prize)** will bring you PEACE!

Reflect:

1. How do I feel about my faith in God? Is it weak or strong?
2. Am I willing to step out in faith and ask the Lord to perform miracles in my life?
3. Do I feel good that Mary and Jesus are on the journey with me? How often do I speak with them?
4. How many times have I tried unsuccessfully to stop worrying? Does this make me feel discouraged?
5. Do I believe that, with the Lord's help, I can overcome anxiety? Am I too proud to ask for his help?

Respond:

Thank you, Jesus, for accompanying me on the journey from fear to faith. Help me remember your presence and turn to you often. Although I am weak, I believe your grace can allow me to stop worrying. Grant me the strength to continue the journey and increase my desire to grow close to you. Amen.

10

Do What You Can (*Prepare*)

I n this chapter, we'll look at the first of the 5 P's of Peace—
Prepare. One of the greatest sources of worry is the fear of
the unknown. Most of us know what it's like to worry about
what may happen to ourselves or to our loved ones in the future.
We also tend to worry about upcoming events, generally dwelling on what *could* go wrong. When you begin to feel anxious,
especially about the future, the first question to ask yourself is:

Can I do anything to prepare?

In most cases, there is something you can do to minimize the
potential damage of the fear-producing event. If you are nervous
about failing a test, you can study. If you are worried about having
a heart attack, you can start eating healthier food. If your company
is struggling and you are worried about losing your job, you can
update your résumé and begin looking for a new job. If you're
worried about your basement flooding when you hear a forecast
for heavy rain, you can clean out your gutters. If you're worried
about providing for your family in the event of your death, you
can purchase life insurance. If you are worried you may not go
to heaven because of a serious sin that you have committed, you
can go to confession. I could list many other examples, but I'm
sure you get the point. Preparation, or "doing what we can," is a
great way to decrease our anxiety level.

The phrase, "God helps those who helps themselves" is a well-known reminder that God doesn't expect us to sit back and wait for him to solve all our problems. Rather, he wants us to do what we can and then he will supplement our efforts. While not directly found in the pages of sacred Scripture, the concept advocated by this saying is actually quite biblical. Let's look at a few examples, beginning with Jesus' miraculous multiplication of the loaves and fish:

> As the day was drawing to a close, the Twelve approached him and said, "Dismiss the crowd so that they can go to the surrounding villages and farms and find lodging and provisions; for we are in a deserted place here." He said to them, "Give them some food yourselves." They replied, "Five loaves and two fish are all we have, unless we ourselves go and buy food for all these people." Now the men there numbered about five thousand. Then he said to his disciples, "Have them sit down in groups of [about] fifty." They did so and made them all sit down. Then taking the five loaves and the two fish, and looking up to heaven, he said the blessing over them, broke them, and gave them to the disciples to set before the crowd. They all ate and were satisfied. And when the leftover fragments were picked up, they filled twelve wicker baskets (Luke 9:12–17).

After reading this passage, did you wonder why Jesus didn't just take care of the food shortage by himself? Sure, he's the one who performed the miracle and multiplied the five loaves and two fish, but the apostles are also given a major role in feeding the crowd. There are some subtle (but important) details in this story that could easily be overlooked, so let's take a closer look at what took place. Did you catch the part when Jesus told the apostles that *they* should give the crowd some food? Why would he instruct them to do that, given that they didn't have enough provisions to feed the crowd? Could it be he wanted them to try their best and trust him with the rest? If you examine this passage carefully, you'll see this is what they did. The result? Jesus came through and the crowd was fed. It's important for us to understand this partnership between the apostles and the Lord, so let's look at what they were asked to do. Jesus asked the apostles to do three things: Give the people something to eat, organize the crowd into groups of fifty, and distribute the bread and fish to the crowd. On the other hand, Jesus' role was to miraculously multiply the loaves and fish. What's great about this story is that, although it didn't seem like it, the apostles ended up having enough food to feed the crowd. The happy ending occurred because they did what they could and trusted Jesus to do the heavy lifting. He then came through with the miracle, and the crisis was solved.

Let's look at another example, once again involving Jesus and his apostles. This encounter took place after the Lord's resurrection. The apostles have temporarily gone back to their lives as fishermen and have just completed an unsuccessful night of fishing. Things would change for the better, however, once Jesus came on the scene.

When it was already dawn, Jesus was standing on the shore; but the disciples did not realize that it was Jesus. Jesus said to them, "Children, have you caught anything to eat?" They answered him, "No." So he said to them, "Cast the net over the right side of the boat and you will find something." So they cast it, and were not able to pull it in because of the number of fish. So the disciple whom Jesus loved said to Peter, "It is the Lord." When Simon Peter heard that it was the Lord, he tucked in his garment, for he was lightly clad, and jumped into the sea. The other disciples came in the boat, for they were not far from shore, only about a hundred yards, dragging the net with the fish. When they climbed out on shore, they saw a charcoal fire with fish on

it and bread. Jesus said to them, "Bring some of the fish
you just caught" (John 21:4–10).

In this example, the apostles are indeed doing something to
help themselves. Unfortunately, their fishing trip was a complete
bust. They spend all night on the sea but catch nothing! For
fishermen who earn their living by catching fish, this is catastrophic. How can they earn a living selling fish if they have
none to sell? Once again, Jesus makes his presence known and
will save the day. And similar to the way he handled the feeding
of the five thousand, Jesus doesn't simply hand them the fish.
Instead, he instructs the men to do something and they obey.
After following Jesus' instructions and casting their nets over
the right side of the boat, they catch so many fish that they can't
even haul in their net. Although it really is Jesus who once again
does the bulk of the work, he refers to the fish as the ones "you
just caught." This is another example of the partnership between
Jesus and man. While both of these Bible passages involve our
Lord's intervention, human participation is necessary. What
would have happened if the apostles refused to follow Jesus'
directions to do what little they could to resolve the situation?
It's likely both of these stories would not have ended on a positive note. When making the journey from fear to faith, Jesus
will help us. It's even safe to say he will do most of the work. He
does expect us, however, to do our part by doing what we can.

In another biblical example, the people of Thessalonica were
falling into the trap of doing nothing and waiting for God to do
all the work. They believed Jesus' Second Coming was imminent
and decided they should just wait for him to arrive. It's easy for
us to realize their approach was wrong. Even though he didn't
possess our 20/20 hindsight, St. Paul knew they were missing the
point. He admonished the people for their idleness and urged
them to continue to work while waiting for the Lord to return.
It is a message that is just as applicable today as it was then:

We instruct you, brothers, in the name of [our] Lord Jesus Christ, to shun any brother who conducts himself in a disorderly way and not according to the tradition they received from us. For you know how one must imitate us. For we did not act in a disorderly way among you, nor did we eat food received free from anyone. On the contrary, in toil and drudgery, night and day we worked, so as not to burden any of you. Not that we do not have the right. Rather, we wanted to present ourselves as a model for you, so that you might imitate us. In fact, when we were with you, we instructed you that if anyone was unwilling to work, neither should that one eat. We hear that some are conducting themselves among you in a disorderly way, by not keeping busy but minding the business of others. Such people we instruct and urge in the Lord Jesus Christ to work quietly and to eat their own food (2 Thessalonians 3:6–12).

The technique of preparation I recommend in this chapter is one that's common to any self-help method designed to reduce anxiety. It is even included in nonreligious plans because it is simply a matter of common sense. If you're worried about something going wrong, it's only logical that you will do anything in your power to prevent it from happening. In our zeal to let God help us, however, we sometimes forget we can also help ourselves. A great piece of advice generally attributed to St. Ignatius of Loyola and included in the *Catechism of the Catholic Church* (CCC 2834) is:

Pray as if everything depended on God and work as if everything depended on you (*CCC* 2834).

In other words, we should ask God to help us (we'll cover this in a future chapter), but we must also try to help ourselves. Although it sounds simple, it takes practice to know where to draw the line. Just how much should I do and how much should God do? How do I know when it's time to let go? Generally speaking, we can determine if we've done all we can by asking ourselves, "Is there anything else I can do?" One important qualification is that, in this first of the five steps, I am only talking about physical things. There are other spiritual steps we can take—and we will discuss them—but for now we're just focusing on physical actions we can take to lessen the chances of a negative outcome. Is there anything else I can do? And, if we're totally honest with ourselves, we generally know when we've done all we can. Unfortunately, it's usually at this point that our anxiety kicks into overdrive! Why? Because we have a hard time turning control over to the Lord. Sad but true, right?

Preparation is a great way to minimize feelings of anxiety. Can I do anything to prepare? Is there anything else I can do? If the answer to these questions is "no," you should feel better knowing that you did your part. Now it's time to look at the remaining spiritual steps, all of which will involve letting God do the bulk of the work!

Remember:

1. God expects us to do what we can to solve our problems.
2. The uncertainty of the future is a leading cause of anxiety.
3. Preparation (doing what we can) is not only a great way to prevent negative outcomes from occurring, but it helps to reduce our anxiety level.
4. The Lord can (and will) multiply the fruit of our work.
5. Once we have taken every physical action to solve our problems, it's time to move on to the spiritual steps.

Reflect:

1. Do I feel anxious even after I've done all I can to solve my problems?
2. Does my anxiety level increase once I have done all I can and need to trust in God's providence?
3. Do I sometimes lie awake at night worrying about what may happen in the future?
4. The Bible contains numerous examples of miracles. Do I believe Jesus can perform miracles in my life? If my answer is "no," why not?
5. When it comes to my life, am I ready to do *my* job and let God do *his* job?

Respond:

When faced with anxiety, Lord, help me to remember I should do all I can to resolve the issue. Once I have done that, grant me the grace to turn control over to you. Although I sometimes try to do your job (as well as my own), I will try to trust you more. Please increase my faith in you. Amen.

11

One Day at a Time (*Present*)

We all know what it means to take life one day at a time, but how many of us put it into practice? If you're a worrier, you probably violate this practice at least once every day. Why? Because the future can be a scary place for anyone with a tendency to be anxious. There is a certain element of security in dealing with known issues or problems, but the fear of the unknown can be crippling. In this chapter, we're going to discuss the second of the 5 P's of Peace—**Present**. If we are going to successfully make the journey from fear to faith, *we must learn to live in the present moment!*

Instead of me doing all of the talking (or writing), I'm going to let Jesus get us started. The Lord constantly emphasized the need to focus on the present. In reality, it's all we have. The past is gone and the future is not guaranteed. Let's look at some of Jesus' teachings on this crucial point. We'll begin with Christ's first recorded words in Mark's Gospel:

> "This is the time of fulfillment. The kingdom of God is at hand. Repent, and believe in the gospel" (Mark 1:15).

Note that Jesus is speaking in the present tense. He does not say that the kingdom of God will come and that we should repent and believe at some point in the future. Instead, he declares God's kingdom is here now and our repentance and belief should begin immediately. Reading the Lord's words, even 2,000 years after they were first spoken, it's apparent there is a sense of urgency to his message. Here's another example. This time Jesus is reminding us our lives will come to an end one day, and we will be judged on how well we followed his commands. Once again, he is emphasizing the need to get ready...now!

> Therefore, stay awake! For you do not know on which day your Lord will come. Be sure of this: if the master of the house had known the hour of night when the thief was coming, he would have stayed awake and not let his house be broken into. So too, you also must be prepared, for at an hour you do not expect, the Son of Man will come (Matthew 24:42–44).

Not only does this passage deal with the need to focus on the present, but it reaffirms the importance of the first P of Peace—preparation! Jesus reminds us of the need to do something and do it now! The warning that one day we'll have to account for our actions will be wasted unless we listen and respond NOW! As the Lord so clearly reminds us, we don't know when that day will be. Therefore, we must step into action in the present moment. Now let's take a look at another one of Jesus' instructions, one that deals specifically with worry. Despite the fact his words are crystal clear and etched in most of our minds, we often ignore his command:

> "Do not worry about tomorrow; tomorrow will take care of itself. Sufficient for a day is its own evil" (Matthew 6:34).

In 2002, my father was diagnosed with lung cancer. His illness seemingly came out of the blue and was discovered through a routine chest X-ray. He was having some problems with an irregular heartbeat, contacted his doctor, and was instructed to visit the hospital emergency room. When he arrived at the hospital, it was discovered that my father had a mass on his lung. Since he quit smoking forty years earlier, we were stunned by the finding. Within two days, it was confirmed that he not only had lung cancer but that it had spread to his bones. It was decided that my father would be treated with a combination of radiation and chemotherapy. Although his prognosis was not good, the doctors felt treatment could possibly bring some relief. Immediately my mind began to race as I thought of what the future could bring. My father was seventy-nine years old, and my mother was in the beginning stages of dementia.

I worried what would happen to my mother, who would no longer be able to live alone. I began to grieve as I thought about the void my father's death would bring. My heart began to sink as I anticipated the suffering he would have to endure. And then something happened. I realized I was putting the cart before the horse. In my mind, my father had already died and I was dealing with the fallout from that imaginary death. In what I attribute to the prompting of the Holy Spirit, I suddenly understood my approach was all wrong. By focusing on my father's death, I was failing to enjoy time with him while he was still alive.

From that day forward, my routine changed drastically. I prayed for his healing, but I also prayed for the grace to live one day at a time. This grace arrived quickly, and I was able to suppress the thoughts of what *might* happen as his illness progressed. Whenever I could, I visited Dad and did the things we used to do. We watched football, talked about my job, and just enjoyed being with one another. On the days when I couldn't see him in person, I would call him on the phone and chat. I still remember how comforting it was to hear him pick up the phone and say, "Hello." At that moment, I was living completely in the present and I was happy my father was alive and could speak to me. I'd ask, "How are you, Dad?" and he'd reply, "Pretty good. How about you?" Judging by our phone conversation, everything seemed normal. Even though my father was very sick, we enjoyed a nice daily routine. Dad and I were growing closer to one another. In spite of the circumstances, it was a pleasant time.

On Friday, August 30, 2002, I went to visit my father, and we watched a football game. Our Philadelphia Eagles were playing the New York Jets in the final game of the preseason. The Eagles lost, and we joked about how bad they were (in Philly, we love to complain about our sports teams). After the game I shook my Dad's hand, said "goodbye" and told him I'd talk to him on Saturday. As always he said, "Take care, Gar." The next evening I was sitting at home watching TV with my family when the phone rang. My mother told me that my father was having trouble breathing and an ambulance was taking him to the hospital. By the time my sister and I arrived at the emergency room, my father had died. Apparently, he died suddenly while sitting in his favorite chair, enjoying a visit with some close friends. Little did I know that when I said "goodbye" to Dad the previous evening, it was the last time I would see him alive.

In hindsight, my prediction for my father's future was completely wrong. Instead of him wasting away and suffering as the cancer ravaged his body, he died of a sudden heart attack one month after his diagnosis. If I had spent all my time focusing on the suffering I thought was headed his way and preparing for life after he died, I would have missed one of the best months Dad and I ever spent together. Although my father and I were always somewhat close, we never spoke on a daily basis until the last month of his life. One of the biggest mistakes we can make is to worry about what *may* happen in the future. Not only do we usually get it wrong, but it causes us to miss out on the present.

In an effort to live in the present moment, we must learn to forget the "what ifs." So many times we make the mistake of worrying about imaginary problems. When we look back over the course of our lives, we realize most of these problems or negative outcomes never occurred.

What if I lose my job?

What if my husband/wife dies?

What if I fail this test?

What if I never get married?

What if I'm not good enough to go to heaven?

Worrying about the "what-ifs" is a completely unproductive use of your time. Doing something about the "what-ifs," on the other hand, is another story. As discussed in the previous chapter, updating your résumé, buying life insurance, and studying for an upcoming test are productive responses to some of the above concerns. Worrying about things that may not happen doesn't do any good. When we worry about suffering that may come our way, we are ignoring one important fact. The Lord is always there for us. There's an old saying that expresses this sentiment well:

If God Brings You to It, He Will Bring You Through It!

While the source of the quote is unknown, the message is right on the money. God will not allow anything to happen to us (even the most intense suffering) without giving us the grace to endure it. On the other hand, he won't give us the grace to deal with imaginary problems. Why should he? They aren't real problems! When we look at the sudden death of a co-worker's wife or a friend's lengthy period of unemployment, we sometimes cringe and think we could never handle something like that. The reason we feel that way is because God doesn't give us the grace to deal with the problems of others. If these were our problems, we would receive the grace to manage them.

If you can learn to live in the present moment and to forget the "what-ifs," you'll be well on your way to achieving peace in your daily life. In the next chapter, we'll focus on the most effective thing we can do when faced with a problem:

Ask God for help!

Remember:

1. If we worry about the future, we lose sight of the present.
2. Living in the present moment is one of the keys to achieving peace in our lives.
3. Most of the things we've worried about have never happened.
4. Forgetting about the "what ifs" is necessary for living one day at a time.
5. God does not give us the grace to deal with imaginary problems.

Reflect:

1. Do I worry about things that may happen in the future?
2. Why do I worry about future events? Am I afraid to suffer?
3. Think of things you've worried about in the past. Did they ever occur? If they did occur, were they as bad as you thought they would be?
4. Did you ever feel the Lord's presence when you were going through a difficult situation?
5. If God allows suffering to enter your life, do you believe he will assist you?

Respond:

Dear Jesus, please help me to take one day at a time. Thank you for the gift of today, as I realize it is all I am guaranteed. Allow me to better appreciate the present and help me to respond to your call. When I begin to worry about the future, help me to focus on you instead. Please continue to remain with me always. Amen.

12

Ask For Help (*Pray*)

Conversion (growing closer to the Lord) should not be a one-and-done experience. Instead, it should be an ongoing process that lasts throughout our life. While my major conversion occurred in late 2004, I had many mini-conversions going back to when I was still in grade school. I suspect many of you can relate to that experience. As events unfold, there are times when we grow closer to Christ and times when we move away from him. While we should strive to grow closer to the Lord each day, the typical spiritual journey generally involves wrong turns and bumps in the road. We shouldn't let those "slip-ups" discourage us. Instead, we should simply do our best to get back on track and try to find Jesus in all situations.

Even though I was a lukewarm Catholic (at best!) for the majority of my life, I knew where to find the Lord when I had a problem. As someone who has always been anxiety-prone, I often found myself praying when I was afraid. Although my prayers were simple and generally consisted of asking Jesus to "not let this happen," or "please let this happen," they always delivered immediate results. While he didn't always answer my requests immediately and sometimes even said "no," there was one thing that always happened when I prayed. I felt a sense of comfort. It didn't matter if I was praying for the health of my parents, to meet a girlfriend, or to get a job. I always felt more peaceful after

I finished praying. That was no accident, as one of the immediate effects of prayer is a feeling of peace. Let's now look at the third of the 5 P's of Peace—**Prayer.**

The amazing thing about prayer is that we don't have to fully understand it in order for it to be effective. Even though I was lukewarm, I still knew the Lord could help me with my problems. The fact that it was an act of desperation didn't matter. Jesus continually heard my cries for help and came to my assistance. Please remember this: Every time we pray, something happens. *Every time!* That's an important lesson and one you should never forget. Jesus assures us of this fact in his Sermon on the Mount.

> "Ask and it will be given to you; seek and you will find; knock and the door will be opened to you. For everyone who asks, receives; and the one who seeks, finds; and to the one who knocks, the door will be opened. Which one of you would hand his son a stone when he asks for a loaf of bread or a snake when he asks for a fish? If you then, who are wicked, know how to give good gifts to your children, how much more will your heavenly Father give good things to those who ask him" (Matthew 7:7–11).

If we ask the Lord for something, he will answer us. Always! His words are clear and there are no exceptions. Unfortunately, we can easily lose sight of this fact and become frustrated when his answer doesn't meet our expectations. If we look carefully at his words, however, Jesus never promised we would get exactly what we requested. Instead, he assures us we will receive what we need. Many times we ask for things that are not good for us. If these requests were granted, they could possibly jeopardize our chances of getting to heaven. Obviously, God loves us too much to let that happen. Therefore, sometimes the answer to our prayer will be "no."

I know what you're thinking. If God is only going to give us things that are good for us, then we better start figuring out how to make that determination. What if we start asking for "bad" things? How do we know if something is bad for us? It's not easy. That new job which pays a great deal of money could require us to spend more time away from our family and cause us to lose our dependence on God. That relationship with the "perfect" man or woman might lead us into mortal sin. The long-desired physical healing could make us stop praying. Many seemingly good things could actually be harmful to our spiritual well-being. So what can we do? If we don't know what is good for us, should we pray for anything? If even "good" things can be "bad," this prayer stuff is becoming way too stressful! Relax. The good news is we don't have to worry about it. We should feel free to ask with confidence for what we think we need, knowing the Lord will not give us anything that can harm us spiritually. Our job is to ask. His job is to provide the appropriate answer. Need an example? Let's look at the prayer of Jesus on the night before he died:

> Then going out he went, as was his custom, to the Mount of Olives, and the disciples followed him. When he arrived at the place he said to them, "Pray that you may not undergo the test." After withdrawing about a stone's throw from them and kneeling, he prayed, saying, "Father, if you are willing, take this cup away from me; still, not my will but yours be done." And to strengthen him an angel from heaven appeared to him (Luke 22:39–43).

The first lesson we can learn from this passage is just how important prayer really is. Immediately following this episode, Jesus is taken into captivity. He will then be put to death. Since he is God, he obviously knew what was about to happen. Therefore, in his last act as a free man, Jesus chose to pray. Thinking about this fact should remove any doubts about the importance of prayer! Of course, an even more obvious reminder of the importance of prayer is the fact that Christ was often found in prayer. If Jesus considered prayer to be important, shouldn't we?

Let's now examine the fact that Jesus was asking for the "cup of suffering" to be taken from him. Without getting overly deep, although Jesus was God, he was able to pray to the Father because they are different persons. The Father, Son, and Holy Spirit are all distinct and can (and do) communicate with one another. By doing this, Jesus gives us an example of how we should pray. Obviously, his suffering was necessary and would result in our redemption. Note that he asks for it to be taken away, but he also adds the words, "still, not my will but yours be done." These words provide us with a great reminder that it is perfectly acceptable to ask for our suffering to be taken away. Furthermore, Jesus' prayer assures us we can pray for anything, even if we're not sure it is good for us. Of course, we shouldn't ask for anything sinful or something that we know can be harmful, but if you're not sure, ask. Just be sure to have the same attitude as Jesus: "Thy will be done!" In other words, when you ask God for something, be ready to accept his answer!

Finally, did you notice what happens in this Bible passage? Jesus asked his Father for the cup of suffering to be taken from him and that did not happen. Basically the answer was "no." This is an absolutely valid answer to our prayers and does in no way violate Jesus' ask-and-you-shall-receive promise. But did you notice what else happened here? Christ received something he didn't ask for. An angel was sent from heaven to strengthen him. When we pray, the Lord will respond with what we need. Even if we're unaware of our "real" needs, God knows what they are and will respond appropriately.

Now that we know the importance of prayer and understand it's OK to pray for what we think we need, let's look at another common question. How long should I keep praying for the same intention before the Lord gets tired of hearing from me? Once again, the answer can be found in the Bible. First, let's look at Matthew's version of the Agony in the Garden. While it's similar to Luke's (as discussed above), it contains some unique details:

> He advanced a little and fell prostrate in prayer, saying, "My Father, if it is possible, let this cup pass from me; yet, not as I will, but as you will." When he returned to his disciples he found them asleep. He said to Peter, "So you could not keep watch with me for one hour? Watch and pray that you may not undergo the test. The spirit is willing, but the flesh is weak." Withdrawing a second time, he prayed again, "My Father, if it is not possible that this cup pass without my drinking it, your will be done!" Then he returned once more and found them asleep, for they could not keep their eyes open. He left them and withdrew again and prayed a third time, saying the same thing again (Matthew 26:39–44).

Jesus asked for the same thing three times, using the same words. If it's good enough for Jesus, it's good enough for us. Keep asking! God will never get tired of hearing from you. Here's another example that comes directly from a parable told by Jesus.

> Then he told them a parable about the necessity for them to pray always without becoming weary. He said, "There was a judge in a certain town who neither feared God nor respected any human being. And a widow in that town used to come to him and say, 'Render a just decision for me against my adversary.' For a long time the judge was unwilling, but eventually he thought, 'While it is true that I neither fear God nor respect any human being, because this widow keeps bothering me I shall deliver a just decision for her lest she finally come and strike me.'" The Lord said, "Pay attention to what the dishonest judge says. Will not God then secure the rights of his chosen ones who

call out to him day and night? Will he be slow to answer them? I tell you, he will see to it that justice is done for them speedily. But when the Son of Man comes, will he find faith on earth?" (Luke 18:1–8).

What can we learn from this parable? Luke tells us all we need to know in the first line. Keep on praying and don't give up! What about the dishonest judge? Jesus uses this example in order to get our attention. This judge is the complete opposite of our heavenly Father and yet he gives in to the persistence of the widow. Can you imagine how much more responsive a loving God will be to our persistent prayers? Don't ever stop asking, brothers and sisters. Your persistence will pay off!

Before we move on to the next chapter, I want to share one final thought about prayer. We often think of prayer as requesting things from God. In reality it's much more than that. The *Catechism* provides a great definition of prayer in the form of a quote from St. John Damascene.

Prayer is the raising of one's mind and heart to God or the requesting of good things from God (*CCC* 2559).

As discussed, developing a close personal relationship with Jesus Christ is the secret to making the journey from fear to faith successfully. That relationship cannot flourish without daily prayer. Continue to ask Jesus for what you need, tell him your thoughts and concerns, and just let him know that you love him. Do it every day and you'll have the third P of Peace covered!

Remember:

1. We don't have to fully understand prayer in order for it to be effective.
2. If we ask the Lord for something, we will receive something.
3. A feeling of peace is often the first fruit of our prayers.
4. We should not hesitate to ask God for anything, unless we know it's sinful or bad for us.
5. Prayer is more than just asking the Lord for something. It is a conversation with him.

Reflect:

1. Do I pray every day?
2. Do I always pray when I am worried?
3. Am I willing to accept the Lord's answer to my prayers, even if it's "no?"
4. Have I ever prayed for one thing and received something else? Do I try to see God's providence in everything that occurs in my life?
5. Do I stop praying if I feel that God is not answering me fast enough?

Respond:

Thank you, Lord, for being available for me always. I know you never tire of hearing from me, and I will continue to speak to you often. Please help me to trust in your providence and to better accept your answers to my prayers. Amen.

13

Turn to the Church (*Participate*)

In the 1980s, a major credit-card company introduced a popular slogan: "Membership has its privileges." By signing up for our credit card, the company implied, you will receive benefits that others will not. The same thing can be said for most organizations, especially those that require a membership fee. For many years, I have been a member of an automobile club that provides emergency roadside assistance. My membership also entitles me to other benefits, such as discounts at hotels and restaurants. There is no doubt membership does indeed have its privileges. As members of the Catholic Church, we have a treasure chest filled with infinite benefits, but we often fail to open up the chest. Let's look at the fourth P of Peace—*Participate*. One of the best things we can do to complete the journey from fear to faith is to participate in all the Church offers.

As we struggle to overcome anxiety, we often focus more on the problem than the solution. As a result, we can spend a great deal of time spinning our wheels and getting nowhere. Fortunately, the Lord is aware of our struggles and doesn't expect us to go it alone. By now, I'm sure you understand Jesus is the answer to any problem you could encounter, and a relationship with him is sure to bring peace into your life. We may not be aware of it, but the most serious problem we could ever face is the possibility of not getting to heaven. Not wanting to leave us stranded, Christ established a Church that provides us with the graces needed to get there. In addition, the graces provided through the Church can also help us to feel peace in our lives. How do we obtain those graces? We can obtain them by participating in what the Church offers. In this chapter we'll look at the sacraments, the papacy, the Bible, sacramentals, and devotions. Opening our Catholic treasure chest and making use of what's inside is a sure way to experience peace!

The Sacraments

The Church offers us seven sacraments: baptism, confirmation, Eucharist, reconciliation, anointing of the sick, holy orders, and matrimony. In this section, we'll be taking a general look at the sacraments and why they are necessary. Much of the material I'll use comes from the *Catechism of the Catholic Church (CCC)*. For detailed information about each of the sacraments, please consult the *Catechism*.

What are the sacraments?

The sacraments are efficacious signs of grace, instituted by Christ and entrusted to the Church, by which divine life is dispensed to us. The visible rites by which the sacraments are celebrated signify and make present the graces proper to each sacrament. They bear fruit in those who receive them with the required dispositions (*CCC* 1131).

Simply put, we receive grace through the sacraments. Grace is what allows us to grow closer to Christ and, ultimately, to get to heaven. Although we can't see grace, it's something we all need... badly! Grace is what God uses to help us overcome our weakness and sinful tendencies. Sounds too good to be true, doesn't it? While it is absolutely true, there is a catch. The amount of grace we receive is directly proportional to how open we are to receiving it. For years, I received the sacrament of the Eucharist weekly but never thought about the fact that I was having an intimate encounter with Christ. I was not open to the infinite graces that were available to me. As a result, my actions weren't indicative of someone who had a deep personal encounter with Christ each week. As the *Catechism* teaches, the sacraments will bear fruit in those who receive them with the required dispositions. If you don't care about receiving the graces and aren't open to how they work in your life, you will probably waste this great gift. What's the solution? Realize the sacraments are an encounter with Jesus and ask him to allow you to receive and respond to all of the graces that are available!

The Papacy

> "And so I say to you, you are Peter, and upon this rock I will build my church, and the gates of the netherworld shall not prevail against it. I will give you the keys to the kingdom of heaven. Whatever you bind on earth shall be bound in heaven; and whatever you loose on earth shall be loosed in heaven" (Matthew 16:18–19).

When Christ appointed Peter as the head of his Church, he also gave him the authority to make binding decisions. Jesus knew of the challenges we would face and therefore established a visible leader of the Church. That leader is the Holy Father, also known as the supreme pontiff or the pope and has the tremendous responsibility of helping us to get to heaven.

> The Lord made St. Peter the visible foundation of his Church. He entrusted the keys of the Church to him. The bishop of the Church of Rome, successor to St. Peter, is "head of the college of bishops, the Vicar of Christ and Pastor of the universal Church on earth." The Pope enjoys, by divine

institution, "supreme, full, immediate, and universal power in the care of souls" (CCC 936–937).

As Catholics, we are blessed to have the Holy Father with us. Let's face it, life is challenging and the world is a different place than it was during the time of Christ. When we read the Bible, we often have difficulty understanding the customs that are discussed. There is no getting around the fact our generation (and every generation before and after us) poses a unique set of challenges. Every day we are faced with moral dilemmas involving such issues as abortion, same-sex marriage, birth control, and euthanasia. We wonder how to deal with non-Christians and those who belong to different Christian denominations. What is the proper Catholic response to evangelization in a world dominated by the internet and social media?

While we could turn to the Bible, most of these issues are not addressed directly. Without additional guidance, we would be forced to make some tough moral decisions on our own. God loves us too much to let that happen and therefore has given us the gift of the papacy. The voice of the Holy Father, the vicar of Christ, helps us to keep our eyes on the Lord as we navigate through the challenges of life. His visible presence is a great blessing to the Church.

The Pope, Bishop of Rome and Peter's successor, "is the perpetual and visible source and foundation of the unity both of the bishops and of the whole company of the faithful."

"For the Roman Pontiff, by reason of his office as vicar of Christ, and as pastor of the entire Church has full, supreme, and universal power over the whole Church, a power which he can always exercise unhindered" (CCC 882).

The Bible

Does God speak to you? Before you say "no," let's take a minute to look at what the Church says about the Bible.

> Sacred Scripture is the speech of God as it is put down in writing under the breath of the Holy Spirit (*CCC* 81).

This statement, originally taken from Vatican II's *Dei Verbum*, is included in the *Catechism* as a reminder that God speaks to us through the Bible. Even though the words were written by human authors, the Church teaches they were inspired by the Holy Spirit. Therefore, it is valid to say God speaks to us when we read the Bible. Thinking about that before opening the Bible can be extremely powerful. Every time you read sacred Scripture or listen to the readings at Mass, God is speaking directly to you. This is the message I tried to emphasize in *A Worrier's Guide to the Bible* and *Listen to Your Blessed Mother*. Sadly, it is a message many Catholics do not understand. It's possible for the Lord to speak to you every day, and all you have to do is open the Bible. The Church's position on sacred Scripture is clear:

> In Sacred Scripture, the Church constantly finds her nourishment and her strength, for she welcomes it not as a human word, "but as what it really is, the word of God." "In the sacred books, the Father who is in heaven comes lovingly to meet his children, and talks with them."
>
> God is the author of Sacred Scripture. "The divinely revealed realities, which are contained and presented in the text of sacred Scripture, have been written down under the inspiration of the Holy Spirit" (*CCC* 104–105).

You may wonder why I have included the Bible as one of the gifts of the Catholic Church. Don't all Christian denominations believe in the Bible? Here's a little-known fact. Many people don't realize it was the Catholic Church that decided which books were truly inspired by God and should be included in the Bible. Yes, the Bible really is a Catholic book, and without the Church, it would not exist.

> It was by the apostolic Tradition that the Church discerned which writings are to be included in the list of the sacred books. This complete list is called the canon of Scripture. It includes 46 books for the Old Testament (45 if we count Jeremiah and Lamentations as one) and 27 for the New (*CCC* 120).

Sacramentals

Sacramentals are another one of the great gifts offered by the Catholic Church. This often-misunderstood category includes medals, scapulars, holy water, and blessings. While they are similar in nature to the sacraments, sacramentals do not confer grace. Instead, they can prepare us to receive and cooperate with grace received through prayer and the sacraments. Here is the official definition.

> Holy Mother Church has, moreover, instituted sacramentals. These are sacred signs which bear a resemblance to the sacraments. They signify effects, particularly of a spiritual nature, which are obtained through the intercession of the Church. By them men are disposed to receive the chief effect of the sacraments, and various occasions in life are rendered holy" (CCC 1667).

As you strive to grow closer to Christ, don't hesitate to wear medals and obtain blessings. All of these things will help you in your journey from fear to faith. Most of us are painfully aware that we need all of the help we can get. Understanding that is a step in the right direction. Putting that knowledge into practice and utilizing these great gifts from the Church is an even better step!

Devotions

Catholics are well-known for their devotions. Some of the better-known devotions are the Miraculous Medal, Divine Mercy, Total Consecration to Jesus through Mary, the Stations of the Cross and the rosary. The Church encourages these expressions of piety, as they can draw us closer to Christ. Although they can be extremely beneficial, devotions must be used in the way intended by the Church. They must never get in the way of our relationship with the Lord. Devotions and expressions of piety must always lead us closer to Jesus and not away from him.

> Pastoral discernment is needed to sustain and support popular piety and, if necessary, to purify and correct the religious sense which underlies these devotions so that the faithful may advance in knowledge of the mystery of Christ. Their exercise is subject to the care and judgment of the bishops and to the general norms of the Church (*CCC* 1676).

When it comes to the Catholic Church, membership certainly does have its privileges. Just as it's much easier—and faster—to travel twenty miles by car (as opposed to walking), the journey from fear to faith becomes less difficult when we share in the gifts offered by the Church. After all, we're trying to get closer to Christ, so it only makes sense that we should participate more fully in the gifts offered by his Church. Doing so will not only provide us with the grace needed to relieve our anxiety, but will give us what we need to reach heaven. In the next chapter, we'll look at the final step in our journey from fear to faith...the need to keep our eye on the PRIZE!

Remember:

1. Christ instituted the sacraments as a means to give us grace.
2. Jesus is present in each of the seven sacraments.
3. The pope is the successor of St. Peter and is responsible for the care of our souls.
4. The Catholic Church decided which books should be included in the Bible.
5. The use of sacramentals can better dispose us to receive and cooperate with grace.

Reflect:

1. How often do I receive the sacraments of Communion and reconciliation? Do I ask the Lord to receive all of the possible graces associated with these sacraments?
2. Do I obey the instructions of the Holy Father?
3. Do I read the Bible daily, knowing God speaks to me when I do?
4. How important are sacramentals in my life? Do I wear any religious medals or try to obtain blessings whenever possible?
5. What devotions are important to me? Do I avoid devotions completely? If so, wouldn't it be a good idea to investigate some Church-approved devotions?

Respond:

Dear Jesus, thank you for the gift of your Church. Because of your generosity, it isn't necessary for me to make the journey from fear to faith by myself. Whenever I participate in the gifts the Church offers, I know you are right beside me. Please increase my appreciation for your Church's gifts every day of my life. Amen.

14

Focus on Heaven (*Prize*)

Earlier I mentioned the annual trips I took with my best friend, Chuck. From 1982 through 1988, Chuck and I would save our money, choose a destination, and take a yearly vacation. The process would begin in January as we decided on a location and made the necessary reservations. Although the vacation itself was one of the highlights of our year, making the plans was also a big source of enjoyment. Why? Mainly because it helped us to look forward to something pleasant and take our focus off the more stressful parts of the present. At the time, Chuck and I didn't enjoy our jobs and also struggled with the cold weather. Thinking about the fun we would have in the future made the present bearable. As I dealt with the winter chill and struggled through my daily duties as a federal employee, I dreamed of relaxing days and lots of sun in California, Florida, and Hawaii. There was a light at the end of the tunnel, the anticipation of better days. In this chapter, we're going to look at heaven as the ultimate light at the end of the tunnel. The anticipation of this reward can not only get us through the darkest of days but it can bring us great peace.

> "Do not let your hearts be troubled. You have faith in God; have faith also in me. In my Father's house there are many dwelling places. If there were not, would I have told you that I am going to prepare a place for you? And if I go

and prepare a place for you, I will come back again and take you to myself, so that where I am you also may be" (John 14:1–3).

Does that Bible passage comfort you? Are you amazed by Jesus' promise that he is preparing a place for us in heaven? Before you answer, let's look at another scenario. Suppose you were promised an all-expenses-paid vacation to the destination of your choice. This trip was guaranteed and would be scheduled for six months in the future. When you're having a bad day, which of these two promises would bring you more consolation? If you're struggling to get out of bed and go to work, which of these scenarios will be in the forefront of your mind? Probably the vacation, right? Don't feel bad about it. That's how our minds work. For many of us, heaven is an abstract concept and isn't something we think about every day. When you throw in the fact you must first die in order to arrive there, it becomes even less appealing. In its explanation of heaven, the *Catechism* acknowledges that a complete understanding is beyond human understanding.

By his death and Resurrection, Jesus Christ has "opened" heaven to us. The life of the blessed consists in the full and perfect possession of the fruits of the redemption accomplished by Christ. He makes partners in his heavenly glorification those who have believed in him and remained faithful to his will. Heaven is the blessed community of all who are perfectly incorporated into Christ. This mystery of blessed communion with God and all who are in Christ is beyond all understanding and description. Scripture speaks of it in images: life, light, peace, wedding feast, wine of the kingdom, the Father's house, the heavenly Jerusalem, paradise: "no eye has seen, nor ear heard, nor the heart of man conceived, what God has prepared for those who love him" (*CCC* 1026–1027).

If we can somehow learn to appreciate the promise of heaven, however, it can bring us a great deal of peace. Is it possible to desire the joy of heaven? Absolutely; and it's going to be much easier than you think. While we will never be able to completely grasp the magnificence of heaven, we can certainly learn to appreciate and desire it more than we do now. Let's examine the fifth (and final) P of Peace—the *Prize*...heaven!

You've probably heard the expression, "Keep your eye on the prize." It's a reminder that focusing on the finish line makes running the race more bearable. If we can somehow learn to appreciate the joy and promises of heaven, even our most severe problems won't seem too bad. Why? Because we know there's a light at the end of the tunnel. We know there is a finish line to the race. Let's begin by looking at what St. Paul wrote about heaven. As you read his words (and every biblical passage that is included in this book), remember that God is the ultimate author of the Bible. Therefore, any message contained therein is spoken directly from the Lord to you!

> If then you were raised with Christ, seek what is above, where Christ is seated at the right hand of God. Think of what is above, not of what is on earth. For you have died, and your life is hidden with Christ in God. When Christ your life appears, then you too will appear with him in glory (Colossians 3:1–4).

Although it may still not come naturally to you (relax, we'll work on it!), St. Paul is reminding us of the importance of focusing on heaven. While it's easy to get distracted because of our daily problems, heaven is our true home, and we are all destined to live there one day. Keeping that in mind will not only help us cope with our problems, but it will ensure that we do end up getting there! Now let's take a look at Paul's explanation of how heaven compares with life on earth.

Therefore, we are not discouraged; rather, although our outer self is wasting away, our inner self is being renewed day by day. For this momentary light affliction is producing for us an eternal weight of glory beyond all comparison, as we look not to what is seen but to what is unseen; for what is seen is transitory, but what is unseen is eternal (2 Corinthians 4:16–18).

I consider that the sufferings of this present time are as nothing compared with the glory to be revealed for us (Romans 8:18).

The message is clear. The joy of heaven far surpasses any happiness we can experience on earth. Additionally, we're told any suffering we may experience in this life isn't even worth comparing to how good it will be in heaven. Whether you feel it or not, that is a strong statement and one we should keep in mind. The unexpected illness, the sudden job loss, loneliness, relationship problems, flat tires, bad weather, whatever...they will all be gone one day. We will not take these earthly burdens with us when we die. Heaven, which lasts forever, will be so much better than anything we'll experience in this life we shouldn't even try to compare. Are you starting to desire it a little? Hang in there, because I'm not done yet. In his Second Letter to the Corinthians, St. Paul elaborates more about the joy of heaven:

For we know that if our earthly dwelling, a tent, should be destroyed, we have a building from God, a dwelling not made with hands, eternal in heaven. For in this tent we groan, longing to be further clothed with our heavenly habitation if indeed, when we have taken it off, we shall not be found naked. For while we are in this tent we groan and are weighed down, because we do not wish to be unclothed but to be further clothed, so that what is mortal may be swallowed up by life. Now the one who has prepared us

for this very thing is God, who has given us the Spirit as a
first installment So we are always courageous, although we
know that while we are at home in the body we are away
from the Lord, for we walk by faith, not by sight. Yet we
are courageous, and we would rather leave the body and
go home to the Lord. Therefore, we aspire to please him,
whether we are at home or away. For we must all appear
before the judgment seat of Christ, so that each one may
receive recompense, according to what he did in the body,
whether good or evil. (2 Corinthians 5:1–10)

The majority of our worries have to do with temporal (or
worldly) things. I travel around the country speaking about
overcoming anxiety and meet many people who are worried.
Without a doubt, the top sources of anxiety are financial and
health issues. While we know that these things are important,
we also know that we're all going to die one day and leave our
possessions behind. In this Bible passage, St. Paul reminds us
that this life is temporary. Remember that all of the earthly problems we face—including financial and health issues—are also
temporary. While that may not instantly make you feel better as
you struggle to pay your mortgage or deal with chemotherapy,
thinking about this message can truly make your struggles
bearable. One of the reasons it's so important to read the Bible
is because it allows God to speak to you. If you read God's word
on a daily basis, you will be changed by his words. Try reading
the above verse a few more times, slowly and prayerfully, and
see if you start to feel a bit more peaceful. I predict that you will.
Let's now take a look at another biblical passage. When Jesus first
told the apostles of his upcoming passion, Peter rejected the idea
and was immediately rebuked by the Lord (Matthew 16:21–23).
Jesus then explained it was necessary for his followers to pick
up and carry their cross. You can probably imagine how they
were feeling after receiving all of this grim news. Knowing that

they needed a boost, it was time for them to receive a vision of the joy of heaven.

> After six days Jesus took Peter, James, and John his brother, and led them up a high mountain by themselves. And he was transfigured before them; his face shone like the sun and his clothes became white as light. And behold, Moses and Elijah appeared to them, conversing with him. Then Peter said to Jesus in reply, "Lord, it is good that we are here. If you wish, I will make three tents here, one for you, one for Moses, and one for Elijah." While he was still speaking, behold, a bright cloud cast a shadow over them, then from the cloud came a voice that said, "This is my beloved Son, with whom I am well pleased; listen to him." When the disciples heard this, they fell prostrate and were very much afraid. But Jesus came and touched them, saying, "Rise, and do not be afraid." And when the disciples raised their eyes, they saw no one else but Jesus alone (Matthew 17:1–8).

In a similar way, meditating on the joy of heaven can help us get through even the most difficult of days. If you're still not feeling it, I recommend you continue to read the Bible verses contained in this chapter. Doing so will allow you to better appreciate the happiness that awaits you in the heavenly kingdom. Also, don't forget to ask the Lord to help you acquire a greater desire for heaven. Now, in order to hold you over until that desire arrives, let's look at it in simple terms. Think about a life without aches and pains, financial problems or bad weather. Think about a big party with all of your best friends, both living and deceased. Imagine a buffet overflowing with your favorite entrees and desserts. As if this isn't good enough, this celebration will be held at the location of your choice. It could be in your favorite vacation spot or your hometown. Everything, and I mean everything, about this party is perfect. And, contrary to the popular expression telling us that all good things must come to an end, this celebration will not have an end. Multiply the joy you feel by a billion and you'll have a tiny bit of the joy that you'll feel in heaven. When you're feeling down and don't know how you'll make it through the day, spend some time thinking about it.

> Then I saw a new heaven and a new earth. The former heaven and the former earth had passed away, and the sea was no more. I also saw the holy city, a new Jerusalem, coming down out of heaven from God, prepared as a bride adorned for her husband. I heard a loud voice from the throne saying, "Behold, God's dwelling is with the human race. He will dwell with them and they will be his people and God himself will always be with them [as their God]. He will wipe every tear from their eyes, and there shall be no more death or mourning, wailing or pain, [for] the old order has passed away." (Revelation 21:1–4)

No worries, no problems, total happiness with God. Forever. That's what heaven is all about!

Remember:

1. Today will come to an end and so will our earthly problems. Heaven, on the other hand, is permanent.
2. The Bible tells us we can't imagine the joy we will feel in heaven.
3. The majority of our worries have to do with temporal (earthly) things.
4. We should ask the Lord to increase our desire for heaven.
5. Focusing on the joy of eternal life with God can help us to endure even the worst trials.

Reflect:

1. How important is heaven to me? Do I think about it every day?
2. Try to remember a peaceful time in your life. It could be a vacation, a time when your children were young, or some other time when all was going well. Recall just how good it felt. Would you like to feel that peace again?
3. Do you ever experience a strong sense of peace when you pray? Imagine if it could last forever.
4. What are your biggest sources of anxiety? Will they matter 100 years from now?
5. Visit a cemetery (physically or in your mind) and think about the people buried there. They are unaffected by health issues or financial problems. Ultimately, the only thing that matters in this life is that we get to heaven. What are you doing to make that a reality?

Respond:

Thank you, Father, for preparing a place for me in heaven. I am extremely grateful you sent your Son to redeem me and allow me to live with you forever once my earthly life is over. Please help me to acquire a greater desire for heaven and to live my life in such a way that it will become a reality for me. Amen.

15

There Is a Reason
(Dealing With Suffering)

Before bringing this book to a close, I would be remiss if I didn't address the number one nemesis to most worriers—suffering. Even though you now have a method (**the 5 P's of Peace**) to deal with anxiety, suffering is the most likely reason you will slip up and begin worrying again. Therefore, it warrants a closer look. Whether it's ongoing or anticipated, suffering (or fear of suffering) can be a cause of sleepless nights for many people. Try to imagine the peace you would feel if you weren't afraid to suffer. When you get right down to it, most of us are afraid of suffering. While I can't promise the techniques offered in this book will free you from suffering (they won't), I will promise that Jesus can bring you peace in the midst of your suffering...if you let him. A deeper understanding of suffering can also make it less frightening. Let's look at why we must suffer, how we can deal with our suffering, and how we can experience peace even when faced with great difficulties.

Why do we have to suffer? Simply put, there is suffering in this life because this world is not heaven. Although it wasn't part of God's original plan, Adam and Eve's sin brought suffering and death into the world. Until we make it to heaven, we are going to experience some degree of unpleasantness every day. Over the course of our lives, however, most of our trials will be relatively minor. Upset stomachs, tiredness, car problems, bad weather, traffic jams, tough days at the office, and many other inconveniences are all part of our earthly life. There are also more severe forms of suffering such as the death of family and friends, serious illness, extreme loneliness, catastrophic financial problems and acts of violence. Followers of Christ are not immune to this reality of life. In fact, Jesus and those closest to him suffered greatly. A closer look at the lives of the Holy Family, the apostles and the saints will reveal that their lives were full of difficulties and pain. We are all going to experience a certain amount of difficulties in our lives. As followers of Jesus, however, we have an edge. Our suffering can have meaning. Furthermore, with the Lord's help, it can even become sweet.

I'm sure you've heard the expression, "every cloud has a silver lining." This is especially true when it comes to suffering. First, let's take a look at a few hypothetical examples of painful situations. A friend informs you that he is going to call you at 3 AM every night for the next year. Your wife declares that, instead of your usual beverage, you'll both be drinking pickle juice with your dinner each night. An email circulated at your office bears the news that from now on there will be no more heat or air conditioning in the company buildings. Wait a minute, you're probably thinking, these are silly examples and don't make any sense. While they might seem silly, could you imagine if you really had to endure these inconveniences? While they are painful in and of themselves, these acts would become more painful because there's no reason for them. On the other hand, how about if you're awakened each night because your crying baby needs to be fed or have his diaper changed? What if you knew the bitter-tasting medicine that made you gag was actually helping you to get better? What if regulating the heating and air conditioning at the office was a cost cutting measure that might allow your company to stay in business? Unlike the first set of examples, in the second set you're being asked to suffer for a reason. Your suffering has meaning. That knowledge makes the pain easier to endure. As Catholics, we believe there is always a reason for our suffering and we can always put it to good use. Through the words of St. Paul, God tells us he can bring good out of any situation.

> We know that all things work for good for those who love God, who are called according to his purpose (Romans 8:28).

This is one of my favorite Bible verses and one you should remember. No matter what you're going through in life, there is a reason. Furthermore, you can rest assured that God is allowing it to happen. While we often can't control the suffering that enters our life, we can control how we respond to that suffering. A proper response on our part can even bring us closer to Christ. And since growing closer to the Lord (and experiencing his peace) is the main theme of this book, let's look at what Jesus has to say about the subject:

> Then he said to all, "If anyone wishes to come after me, he must deny himself and take up his cross daily and follow me" (Luke 9:23).

Jesus isn't telling us that we need to suffer much in order to follow him. Instead, he instructs us that we need to "take up our cross." In other words, he calls us to embrace our suffering. Why? Because it has meaning, and great good can come from it. In his Letter to the Colossians, St. Paul explains the radical concept of redemptive suffering:

> Now I rejoice in my sufferings for your sake, and in my flesh I am filling up what is lacking in the afflictions of Christ on behalf of his body, which is the church (Colossians 1:24).

Without going into a deep theological explanation, let's unpack the idea of redemptive suffering. Because we are part of his mystical body (the Church), Christ allows us to share in his suffering. And not just any suffering, but the suffering that was used to redeem humanity. While there was nothing lacking in the sacrifice of Jesus on Calvary (despite St. Paul's confusing terminology), you and I are invited to unite our suffering with Christ's and to share in his mission. This is the reason behind the familiar expression "offer it up." Anytime we suffer (either in a small or large way), Jesus invites us to climb up on the cross and assist him in the redemption of mankind. Understanding that concept allowed St. Paul not just to accept, but to rejoice in his suffering. While most of us aren't at St. Paul's level of awareness, knowing our suffering can be put to good use can certainly ease the pain a bit.

Additionally, Jesus doesn't expect us to carry our crosses alone. He never said we should pick up our cross and follow our own path. Instead, he tells us to follow him. The Lord is not asking us to do anything he did not do. We all know just how much he suffered, not only on Calvary but throughout his life. He was rejected, threatened, humiliated, and ultimately murdered. When we willingly carry our cross, we imitate Jesus and grow closer to him. Every time we suffer, we are invited to unite our agony with his. As a result, he will not only grant us peace but will take our pain and use it to save souls.

I know that some of this information can be hard to take, especially if you're in the midst of intense suffering. If you're struggling to make sense of your pain, you may need to read this chapter a few times and ask the Holy Spirit to guide you to a deeper understanding. That's a good thing because it helps you to develop a closer relationship with the Lord. Reading the Bible and praying are two of the suggestions I discussed earlier, and this practice will keep you close to Jesus. Keep at it. The understanding and peace will come. How about if it's not coming fast enough? What can you do if you feel like you're at the end of your rope? I know that some of you probably feel this way. I often meet people who feel they are being pushed beyond their limit. They feel that God is asking too much of them. Although it may seem like it, this is never the case. I've been there and I know that feeling, but the Lord will never give us more suffering than we can handle. I'll close this chapter with a Bible verse that will assure us this is the truth. Once again, it is penned by someone who suffered a great deal (St. Paul) but could see God's hand in that suffering. No matter what you are asked to endure, know that the Lord is with you and is ready to come to your assistance.

> God is faithful and will not let you be tried beyond your strength; but with the trial he will also provide a way out, so that you may be able to bear it (1 Corinthians 10:13).

Cry out to him and ask for help. Ask for enlightenment and peace. Never give up because, when you carry your cross, you are not only growing closer to Jesus, you are imitating him.

Remember:

1. God can bring good out of all suffering.
2. Nothing happens to us without the Lord's approval. He is never surprised by the events in our lives.
3. Jesus, Mary, Joseph, the apostles, and the saints suffered a great deal.
4. God will never give us more suffering than we can handle.
5. When we carry our cross, we imitate Jesus.

Reflect:

1. How am I handling the suffering in my life? Am I carrying my cross or complaining?
2. Knowing that Jesus only allows me to suffer if it is good for me, do I ever think about how he feels when I complain? Do you think that makes him sad?
3. How have I reacted to the inconveniences I've experienced in the past twenty-four hours?
4. Try to imagine how difficult it must have been for the Holy Family during the time of Jesus' birth. Picture what Jesus endured as he suffered in the Garden of Gethsemane and as he died on the cross. How do my problems compare with his?
5. Do I try to assist others who are suffering? Who can I help today?

Respond:

Dear Lord, St. Paul assures me that you will never give me more suffering than I can bear, but sometimes I struggle to believe it. Please help me to trust that you are always there for me and will help me to carry my cross. I unite all of my suffering with yours and ask that you use it to save souls. Jesus, I trust in you. Amen.

16

Moving Forward
(*Where Do We Go From Here?*)

So how do you feel now that we've made it through the book? Your worries are all gone, right? Relax...I'm just kidding! While I wouldn't expect your anxiety to be gone, I suspect you may feel a greater sense of hope that you can win the battle. And you can. God does not want you to be anxious. Really! That fact is driven home numerous times in the pages of the Bible, especially by St. Paul, who writes, "I should like you to be free of anxieties" (1 Corinthians 7:32). It's difficult to misinterpret that message. The Lord wants you to trust him with a childlike faith. He desires you to be at peace.

As I stressed several times throughout this book, we shouldn't try to do this alone. In fact, we shouldn't even try to do the bulk of the work. That is the Lord's job. Our job is to do what little we can (remember the 5 P's of Peace) and stay close to Jesus and Mary. If you're like me, you've been trying to do it alone for many years. Even if you have turned to the Lord for help, you were still probably trying to do most of the work. And I bet you have discovered (like me) that you can't just force yourself to stop worrying. For the vast majority of us, it simply doesn't work. If you follow the steps described in this book, however, your worrying will decrease naturally as you grow closer to Jesus.

He really does have that kind of effect on us. The Bible is filled with stories of people being healed (physically and spiritually) by Christ. What's stopping us from running into his arms and experiencing the same results? You guessed it. We stop ourselves. Hopefully, you are now ready to make the journey from fear to faith by entrusting your life to the Lord. The Bible sums it up nicely when we're instructed to "cast all your worries upon him (Jesus) because he cares for you" (1 Peter 5:7).

Try to remember that the journey from fear to faith is not a trip that you'll make once in your life. Although I discussed this before, it warrants another mention. You may be making this journey (using the same steps) every day for the rest of your life and there's nothing wrong with that. In fact, you shouldn't be surprised if you find yourself making the trip several times a day. Again I say, there's nothing wrong with that. Turning to Jesus several times each day (for whatever reason) is not a bad thing. It is a very good thing! You may also discover that, although you find yourself frequently making the journey from fear to faith, it takes less and less time to complete. Your peace may arrive more quickly than in the past. That's a good sign and is an indication that your faith is growing.

Now that you have a game plan to eliminate anxiety, I want to stress one important point. In certain cases, it is possible the techniques listed in this book will not completely relieve your anxiety. Anxiety can have a biological component, and professional help is sometimes necessary. This can involve medication or other therapy. If you fall into this category, do not feel defeated. I would encourage you to seek professional help while continuing to practice the 5 P's of Peace. Seeking the advice of a professional does not eliminate God from the journey but is simply part of the "do what you can" process. In my case, medication was not the answer. I have been able to overcome my anxiety through spiritual means alone. For some people, however, medication and therapy may be necessary. If you feel that you may need some extra help, I strongly recommend that you visit CatholicTherapists.com for a list of professionals who combine psychological healing with the Catholic faith.

Finally, I would like to let you know I will be praying for everyone who reads this book. Therefore, since you're reading it, I'm praying for you! I will ask the Lord to help you break free from anxiety and feel his peace. Furthermore, I will ask Our Lady to intercede for you each day. Know that many graces are heading your way and that you are not fighting the battle alone. I would also invite you to pray for me and everyone who reads this book. That will ensure we all have plenty of prayers as we continue to make the journey from fear to faith. As I travel around the country speaking at parishes and conferences, I hope we get to meet in person. Until then, know that we are all making this journey together, moving from fear to faith along with Jesus and Mary. We *can* win the battle. Keep moving forward, one day at a time. Peace is closer than you think!

> Have no anxiety at all, but in everything, by prayer and petition, with thanksgiving, make your requests known to God. Then the peace of God that surpasses all understanding will guard your hearts and minds in Christ Jesus (Philippians 4:6–7).

About the Author

Gary Zimak is a Catholic speaker, lay evangelist, and radio host. In addition to hosting *Following the Truth* on Blog-TalkRadio, Gary is a regular guest on EWTN Radio's *Son Rise Morning Show, Catholic Connection* with Teresa Tomeo, *Catholic Answers Live,* and Relevant Radio's *Morning Air.*

You can hear Gary's radio show on **BlogTalkRadio** from 8 to 9 PM EST daily or download the podcast from **blogtalkradio.com.** For a list of upcoming shows, speaking engagements, or to request Gary to speak at your next event, visit his website: **followingthetruth.com.**